Words From the Café

An Anthology

Words from the Café provides a glimpse of the magic that takes place each week, in the Safe Place Writing Circle, at Seattle's Recovery Café, when people come together to write and share writing. The range of human experience contained in these pages flies in the face of prevailing stereotypes of people struggling with addiction or mental illness or homelessness. There's no one-size-fits-all identity. Here are people discovering their own unique voices and ways of shaping language to write stories and poems as a way of reclaiming their lives:

"Safe Place writing has been a class in which I have been able to separate from the noise inside my head . . . the quiet is most inviting . . . ."

"I have never had a better writing teacher, or teacher of any kind . . . Because of Anna's inspiration, skill, and her undying belief in us all, I write better here than on my own . . . ."

"I feel very safe to express myself without the fear of being shunned."

"Safe Place is special because the class assumes you have something to say, gives you the benefit of the doubt, and responds to your work non-judgmentally."

"When I'm in the class I feel alive. Discovering I'm a good writer has helped me in other aspects of my life . . . Being appreciated for my humor has also been a welcoming benefit."

"I keep coming back because I love writing. It gets me out with the community and mingling with other aspiring writers."

"You made me feel included in the human race through your writing classes, and your endearing personal spirit."

Words From the Café

An Anthology

Edited by

Anna Bálint

Raven Chronicles Press
Seattle, Washington

Published by Raven Chronicles Press, Shoreline, Washington

Names: Bálint, Anna, editor.
Title: Words From the Café: an anthology / Anna Bálint
Description: Shoreline, Washington: Raven Chronicles Press [2021]
Identifiers: LCCN 2021904002 | ISBN 978-0-9979468-9-5 (paperback) |
ISBN 978-1-7354780-0-5 (ebook)

Cover Art: Photograph by Ginny Banks.
Featured Writers Portraits: Photographs by Willie J. Pugh.
Featured Author Bios: Compiled and written by Anna Bálint.
Editor's Photo: Nick Kazimir.
Book Design: Anna Bálint, Phoebe Bosché, using Palatino (text).
Cover Design: Anna Bálint, Tonya Namura, using Optima (display).
Raven Logo: designed by Scott Martin.

The Raven Chronicles / Raven Chronicles Press is a nonprofit independent publishing press and literary organization, established in Seattle in 1991. We strive to publish and showcase work that embodies the cultural diversity of writers and artists; work that expresses family and forebears; work that connects with the soil, water, and air of place and home.

Raven Chronicles Press
15528 12th Avenue NE
Shoreline, Washington 98155-6226
editors@ravenchronicles.org
https://www.ravenchronicles.org

. . . it has taken me
all of sixty years
to understand
that water is the finest drink,
and bread the most delicious food,
and that art is worthless
unless it plants
a measure of splendor in people's hearts.

—Taha Muhammad Ali

TABLE OF CONTENTS

VI Closing Notes

Foreword

Recovery Café is a community in which all come to know ourselves as valued and loved. It is a place where we can be honest about our pain, vulnerabilities, and brokenness, and invite others into those places where healing is needed. It is a place where we offer our brokenness and our giftedness for the sake of the healing of others. As expressed in our guiding principles, Recovery Café is a place where we can practice new behaviors and practice forgiving ourselves and others when we fall back into unhealthy behaviors. It is a place where we practice compassion and encourage growth. It is a sacred space in which we all seek to live prayerfully, or live from that place of Divine Love in ourselves. It is a place of being both deeply known and loved where others hold us to who we say we want to become.

The Safe Place Writing Circle is a small, intimate, healing community within the larger Recovery Café community. The level of knowing and being known and loving and being loved that takes place in that "safe place" is nothing short of astounding and transformative. You will catch a glimpse of the miracles that take place in that circle as you read the following expressions, and you will likely experience that you are standing on sacred ground.

—*Killian Noe*
Founding Director,
Recovery Café

Introduction:
Safe Place Writing Circle

I share my story, you share your story.
They're not the same story,
but with our stories
we give each other kindness.
—Tamar

In early spring 2012, a friend and long-time student of mine suggested I go with her to have lunch at the Recovery Café and check it out. "It's a great place, and I think you'll really like it. You might even want to teach a class there." At the time I'd barely heard of Recovery Café, even though it turned out I'd driven past it numerous times on my way to drop off my grandson at his Tae Kwon Do classes. Well, it's easy enough to miss if you're not looking for it, wedged as it is into a busy intersection in downtown Seattle, in a low brick building shaped rather like a slice of pie. From the outside, other than its unusual shape, it's a nondescript building. But upon entering, I discovered a light-filled and welcoming space, at the heart of which is an actual café. This serves two free hot meals a day, with a coffee island offering espresso drinks in the afternoon. And there is more: classrooms, meeting spaces, and offices, as well as a good-sized kitchen. The walls are a cheery yellow or brick red, and hung with art.

Recovery Café is a home base of sorts, a place where many different needs are met under one drug- and alcohol-free roof; a place to make friends, socialize, eat, play a card game, attend a recovery circle, use the computer, or sit in an armchair and read quietly. There's a running and walking club, a parent support group, and numerous events to attend. These include an open mike night, presentations by visiting nutritionists and other health professionals, holiday gatherings, and art exhibits. The Recovery Café also has its own school, the School for Recovery, offering a range of classes designed to support recovery and provide learning environments in which people can "grow, heal, discover, take risks, and surprise themselves by doing and becoming what they never thought possible." Classes include a variety of art and creative classes, as well as yoga, meditation and the five elements, life skills courses, and more. The school year is divided into three ten week terms, with a shorter five week term over the summer.

My reaction to all this was yes, yes, yes! I'd love to teach a class here! Sign me up! And so, in spring 2012, I joined the Café community as a volunteer teacher with the School for Recovery. My class was "Writing the Stories We Never Knew Were Ours," which I'd taught a number of times before, at Antioch University and Richard Hugo House. It had been popular in both places, and was similarly well-received at the Café, and I taught back to back classes through the spring and fall terms. By late fall of that same year, my classes had evolved into an ongoing writing circle. This was in response to student feedback and a general clamoring to continue writing their stories.

Today is Friday,
the summer temperature of 76 degrees is great,
Safe Place a refuge . . .
—Taumstar

Since that time, Recovery Café has also been home to Safe Place Writing Circle, and every Friday afternoon (give or take an occasional Café closure for a holiday) people come together to write and share writing. We meet in a light-filled room with windows onto the street on two sides. Outside, the intersecting streets are busy, with buses and a steady stream of traffic. But the windows also frame low branches of trees that grow close to the building, adding a soothing touch of green. A window in a third wall looks out into the Café, where people sit at tables, talk, laugh, drink coffee. Because the windows are double-paned, the sounds from beyond the room are lessened, the roar of buses still audible, but not intrusive. A carpeted floor also contributes to the overall sense of comfort. There is no scraping of chairs, no reverberating or echoey sounds.

Most weeks find between twelve and sixteen of us grouped around several tables pushed together to make one large table. Some weeks our number is more and occasionally less, but it always includes people who have attended regularly over an extended period of a year or more, as well as others who've been coming for a few weeks or months. Often there are also one or two new people, and this is their first or second time of checking us out. Everything begins with greetings, hugs, rearranging of chairs, snippets of news, and always, always laughter. Some people may come in with food trays, having just arrived from an appointment or work, hungry, and barely in time to catch lunch before the kitchen closes up for the afternoon. Others arrive with a mug of coffee, or tea, and maybe someone's brought some cookies. In general it's a happy, comfortable place to be.

I keep coming back because I love writing. —Anonymous

Two basic groups of people seek out Safe Place. Those who already love to write, and those who don't, or don't think they can, but would like to learn how. Either way, they've heard good things about Safe Place, so they check it out. What's to lose? People also come to the group with different degrees of confidence, some still scarred from bad school experiences, or struggling with learning disabilities. But wherever people are at is okay, and it's called "Safe Place" for a reason. From there, all that's needed to get started is pen and paper, a person's words and memories, and a prompt. Soon the most noticeable sound in the room is the scratching of pens on paper.

Recovery is to get back, or return, what was lost.
—Donald

Recovery requires an ongoing commitment of time and energy. There are AA or NA meetings to attend, numerous doctor and therapy appointments, court dates, and the ongoing hassles and red tape that come with agencies such as Veterans Administration and Social Security Administration. There may be disruptions, caused by lack of affordable housing, illness, hospitalizations, or relapse. Signing up for or following through with a ten week writing class may be daunting. The ongoing nature of Safe Place helps accommodate some of these challenges, because it's not going anywhere. It will be there whenever you're ready. There's no need to reserve a spot, or show up every week. Once there, people are free to explore and participate at their own pace. This contributes to the overall feeling of safety, and, in turn, encourages risk taking. Through all this, a sense of community and trust within the group has time to build.

When someone writes stories that grow out of their life experience they discover / rediscover something about themselves in the process. It's a way of reclaiming their life. And that can be very healing. A few minutes before there was a blank sheet of paper. Now there's this. Often what emerges are memories, stories, moments of life that have been buried and forgotten for years. Writing in this way can help make sense of the past while also reaching toward a different future. Reconnecting with lost, or forgotten, moments of joy can help free someone from a tangle of past hurts. This isn't something that's planned or stated as a goal. It just happens.

I don't remember days, I remember moments . . . .

—Johnnie

Other kinds of discoveries also take place. Each person has a unique voice—a way of using language—that has the potential to be beautiful. Discovering that for yourself is immensely powerful. It's in this context that people start to realize well, yes, they can write, and they do have something to say. Or something new to say, or new ways of saying it. They become more inventive—with word play, use of rhythm, metaphor, imagery, detail and dialogue. So there's this continual back and forth, or interweaving, that takes place between story and how language is used, shaped, to tell that story; to capture a particular moment of life, or a belief, or dreams for the future. And every week there are gems.

Don't let it become a burden
write it down
keep it in a safe place.

—Esmeralda

Then there's "the magic" of what happens when these fresh, raw

pieces of writing are shared with the group. The way that different life fragments, mini-stories and recreated moments, resonate and echo one another, often carrying the listeners into other, overlooked memories of their own—with one recreated moment sparking still others. Hearing one another's stories is validating to both author and listener. Knowing that you've created something that others find meaningful, and perhaps beautiful, can be life changing. As is the discovery that your life and experiences resonate and matter to others. And hearing someone else's story can reaffirm something about your own humanity. It all adds up to really being heard, and helps "grow" the overall environment of safety and trust.

You reached into my dark isolation and urged me out with writing . . . —Anonymous

While there is no overarching theme or focus to Safe Place, there is a specific focus to each time we meet, and every week I give a different prompt, often with a handout of two or three poems or short pieces that in some way or other touch on a specific theme. Some weeks a poem comes first, and seems to find me (it feels that way, rather than me finding it), and it's the poem that reveals or suggests a theme. Other times the theme comes first, and has me searching or reaching for poems that embody it. But the prompt might also be a list of song titles, or quotes, or proverbs and sayings. It might be an excerpt from a Ted Talk. Or a video. One time we watched a video of a Lakota Elder telling a personal story about forgiveness. And sometimes the prompt is embodied in a single word or phrase: "Personal Sound Tracks," "The Funny Side of Life," "Thanksgiving on Fridays or Count your Blessings," "Oops! My Mistake!," "The Joy of Movement," "Insects." Occasionally, the weather, or time of year, asserts itself and ends up as a prompt. One such time was "October," accompanied by Donald Hall's poem, "Kicking the Leaves," as a kickoff.

Isn't it amazing how, when you can't think of anything to write, it can all change in an instant! —Steve

From these prompts people write whatever comes. There's no

right or wrong. Usually we write for twenty minutes or so, sometimes longer. The time varies from week to week, determined by group needs. Occasionally someone will say, "I'm not sure I'm doing this right," and I'll answer, "Hey, you're writing. Just go wherever it's taking you. . . ."

Quite often, I don't know what the prompt—or theme—will be until the last minute. Not because I've neglected to plan, but because the "right" themes and prompts tend to reveal themselves if I keep my receptors open. So planning for the week is not primarily a head exercise on my part, but a kind of tuning in, with a lot of intuition involved. Every week, it seems, I'm flying by the seat of my pants in some way or other. Which is fine, as this helps me change direction on the spot if need be, and better respond to whatever comes my way.

Safe Place is the oil to my rusty gears of creativity. —Bang

Overall, Safe Place is more about discovery than instruction, and I see my role as primarily that of facilitator, and "granting," or fostering, permission to speak. As an important part of this I make sure to bring a variety of poetic voices into the room, to speak from within different cultures, different experiences, and from different parts of the world. Some favorites have been Naomi Shihab Nye, Lucille Clifton, Pablo Neruda, Louise Erdrich, Langston Hughes, and Taha Muhammad Ali. Also Rumi, poet and philosopher of the ancient Islamic world.

The relationship between reading and writing, the back and forth between the two, is the main way people develop new writing skills. Some people come to Safe Place with an existing love of poetry and literature and are quite widely read. Most do not, although there are a number of prolific readers of history, philosophy, and other subjects, and in general there is always plenty of knowledge, as well as wisdom, in the room.

Certain poems spark a discussion prior to writing. Rumi's "The Guest House" was one of these, and seemed to suggest that we should invite trouble in the door, as a quest. "The dark thought, the shame, the malice, / meet them at the door laughing, / and invite them in." What did Rumi mean by this? Wasn't inviting trouble in the door kinda risky? "Hey, I've had enough trouble in my life. I don't need any more." But Rumi was insistent: "Welcome and entertain them all! / Even if they're a crowd of sorrows . . . Be grateful for whoever comes . . ."

In the midst of this dark day, I find comfort
in the inner light that I can't ignore. —Mary Jo

A prompt might jump us in any direction. People respond to prompts in different ways, including borrowing a structure—a way of framing and jumping into an idea—from the poem they've just heard / read. For example, Tamar Hirsch's poem "Footprint" takes both its structure and mood / theme from Palestinian poet Taha Muhammad Ali's wonderful poem, "Twigs." This was one of those times when I read, shared a poem without suggesting any particular theme, and instead left things wide open for people to respond to. "What does it say to you? What grabs you? Whatever it is, wherever it takes you, go with it. . . ." This resonated in a number of different ways, with people tapping into the poem's layers of meaning and overlapping themes. This was also one of those times when the language itself stops people in their tracks. The poem speaks to them. Not just because of what it says, but also how it says it; the way that the language fits the meaning, and the meaning inhabits the language. The two seem inseparable. People notice this, comment on it, read a line over again, aloud, and marvel at it. They're inspired, and want to try new things, find new ways of using language.

A wind grazes my skin, whispers in my ear.
'Let me take your pain,' she says. —Angel

The ten featured artists are all long-term members of Safe Place, with between two to four years of attendance. They reflect the overall diversity of the group and of the Recovery Café population as a whole in terms of age, gender, sexual preference, race, ethnicity, level of education and socioeconomic background, as well as the diversity of circumstances that bring people to the Café in the first place. The range of human experience contained in these pages flies in the face of prevailing stereotypes of people struggling with addiction or mental illness or homelessness. There's no one-size-fits-all identity here. The book's inclusion of writing from twelve "other voices" is a reflection of the breadth of participation, and includes a number of long-term but irregular attendees, along with some newer Safe Place writers.

Writing always gives me this feeling
I have grown wings . . . —Anonymous

For the core group of the ten featured writers—selecting and editing work for this book, and going into the recording studio, all expanded the creative process far beyond what is possible in class each week. For most, learning how to revise and edit work was entirely new, and entailed meeting in small groups, or individually, and with quite a bit more direct teaching than happens in class; all of it with the goal of making the entire experience as hands on as possible, encouraging people to take ownership of the entire process of revising, shaping, and "finishing" their work.

In producing the CD, the recording studio meant entering another realm entirely, and gave amplified meaning to the phrase "finding my voice." Preparing for the studio was fun, and completely different from anything that had happened so far. Many years ago, long before I became a writer and teacher, I trained in theatre arts with a focus on acting. This now came in handy. Our small group rehearsals began with tongue twisters and other voice exercises as warm ups, as well as learning to pause for dramatic effect and clarity; we also had timed readings, and gave one another feedback. All of it a lot of fun, but also nerve-wracking for some, with the thought of going into a recording studio still daunting, and a little too exposing perhaps. And how was this safe?

I was nervous too, wanting it to be a good experience for each person, above and beyond the end result. Studio time was scheduled in small groups, and sometimes singly. And every time, by the end of the session, people were elated, rejuvenated—with the experience transformative for each person. Nervousness turned into empowerment and confidence as each person claimed and spoke their own words. Their time in the studio, and the engineer's enthusiasm for their poems and stories, further enhanced their sense of being listened to, valued, taken seriously . . . and the belief that their stories and life experiences had meaning for others beyond the writing circle itself. People came away from the experience with a feeling of, "Yes, I can!" One person, who had been especially nervous, emerged from the studio beaming, face aglow, and declared: "That had to be one of the best times of my entire life!" I was elated too, and privileged to have witnessed each person's transformation, grateful for the opportunity to have played a part in it.

*The idea of doing a book and CD grew out of all this listening and learning, and the desire to share the magic that happens in Safe Place each week. While there is no way to truly capture what takes place within the confines of a book, or a CD, hopefully, they will provide a partial glimpse and understanding. The CD came about as a way of capturing people's actual voices as they read their own work. Which is about as close as it's possible to get to the weekly share-time without actually being there.

—Anna Bálint
Founder and Teacher,
Safe Place Writing Circle,
Recovery Café, Seattle

*CDs were only available in First Edition copies of this book.

Introduction

to the Second Edition

Much has happened in Safe Place Writing Circle since *Words From the Café, an anthology,* was first published in October, 2016. The Trump presidency, with its upheavals, uncertainty, and callous disregard for the needs of vulnerable populations, was an unsettling time for many, including those who attended Safe Place Writing Circle. Yet, through it all, Safe Place continued to flourish and meet on a weekly basis, while also branching out in new directions.

Following publication of the anthology, numerous opportunities opened up for Safe Place, starting with a variety of well-attended public readings and talks. These events, along with sales of the book and its availability at the Seattle Public Library (SPL), led to a growing interest in Safe Place. Venues that have hosted Safe Place writers in the past few years include Elliott Bay Book Co., Jack Straw Cultural Center, the steps of Seattle City Hall, the University of Washington, Columbia City Gallery, the Douglas Truth Library Branch (SPL), and Seattle University.

Alongside these events, Safe Place writing—by both "older" and "newer" Safe Place writers—was making its way into print and out into the world, appearing in both literary publications and community-based recovery newsletters. Through it all, the ebb and flow nature of Safe Place, and the healing "magic" that occurred in the classroom every week, continued. A few of the writers in *Words From the Café* are still with us nearly five years later, which delights me, while most have since moved on to new chapters in their lives—to jobs, training programs, or to attend college or university. Meanwhile, so many new people joined Safe Place at some point during the past few years that there were weeks when the room seemed about to burst at the seams—with some attending briefly, others for several months, while still others evolved into a "new generation" of long-term regulars. And then there were the Safe Place regulars who we lost, one or two lives set back by mental health relapses; others due to the chronic lack of affordable housing in the Seattle area. But the deaths of Donald Butler and Cathy Scott, both much-loved Safe Place regulars, was an especially hard loss.

Donald, one of the ten featured writers in *Words From the Café*, had been a pivotal member of Safe Place from its earliest days. He passed away in March 2018. Cathy Scott, still a fairly new member when her poem appeared as one of the book's "Other Voices," quickly became a treasured mainstay who remained with the group until her death in May 2020. Tragically, both Donald and Cathy died of complications from ongoing medical conditions related to, and exacerbated by, the poverty, trauma, and inadequate health care they experienced for so much of their lives.

Both Donald's and Cathy's writing and images appeared as part of "Writing Trauma: Voices and Faces of Recovery," an exhibit of writing and photographs. This was our last public event before the COVID-19 pandemic shut everything down. It featured ten, mostly newer, Safe Place writers, and remained on public view at the University of Washington's School of Social Work for six weeks—its end date of early March 2020 just happened to overlap with the beginning of the pandemic.

As COVID-19 necessitated that most public spaces and businesses close their doors—including Recovery Café—Safe Place Writing Circle quickly changed gears. Starting mid-March 2020, we switched to meeting up online rather than in person—via email for a couple of months, then switching to the Zoom communications platform. This is how we continue to meet as of this writing. Sadly, a few long-term members were unable to take part in this transition due to difficulties accessing or using computer technology. On the other hand, a few of the people who'd had to move out of the Puget Sound region were now able to rejoin us—precisely because of Zoom. As 2022 approaches, Recovery Café anticipates being able to reopen and make in-person classes available to Safe Place participants once more, while also supporting a hybrid model with a Zoom class for those who prefer, or depend on it.

—*Anna Bálint*
Seattle, December, 2021

I

Featured Writers

Johnnie Powell

Johnnie was a World War II baby, born and raised in New York, New York. He joined Safe Place Writing Circle three years ago, bringing a whole lot of enthusiasm into the room with him. He described himself as never having been any good at writing, but was willing to give it a try. Try he did, and quickly discovered his ability to sing language onto the page.

While Johnnie has lived through some dark times, for the most part he chooses not to revisit these through his writing, preferring to look to a brighter future and celebrate the life he has now. When he does write about his past, it is mostly to return to happy times in his childhood and early years, and claim those good memories as being an essential part of himself. Other times, he may revisit people and moments from his past that taught him something important and helped him to change. Johnnie's overall enthusiasm is infectious, and translates into seeing the positive in others; he can also always be counted on to extend a warm welcome to new people in the group.

One thing that caught my attention in Johnnie's writing, from early on, was his use of inspirational lines and metaphors. Sometimes these are Johnnie originals, and other times he borrows a quote or saying he came across in a book or poem. Either way, he makes it his own because it's one thing to memorize a quote, and another matter to make creative and original use of it in your own writing.

Dreams, where my imagination flies into the future and brings it back to the present.

Johnnie Powell

GAME CHANGER

If you can't fly, then run, if you can't run, then walk, if you can't walk, then crawl, but whatever you do, keep moving forward. You can't have a positive life and a negative mind. With each new day comes new strength and new thoughts. It's kind of fun to do the impossible all day and every day, but so easy. I start by doing what's necessary, then do what's possible, and suddenly I am doing the impossible!

I can't change the direction of the wind, but I can adjust my sails to always, and I say always, reach my destination. Perfection, they say, is not attainable. But if I choose perfection I can catch excellence. Remember, there are two ways of spreading light. To be the candle or the mirror that reflects it. I know who I am. I am a game changer. I'll never give up, knowing that in the right place and time, the tide will turn.

Johnnie Powell

GRANDMOTHER

My grandmother started walking five miles a day when she was sixty. She's ninety-seven now, and we don't know where she is . . . . My grandmother was a piece of work. She used to chew snuff then spit into a pail and never missed. She always seemed to be old, like a piece of ancient history. She talked about picking cotton as a little girl in the South. Her hands looked like pieces of concrete. She reminded me of an iron pillar, sitting in her rocking chair, rocking back and forth. Nothing and no one seemed to bother her.

Her faith in God was her own making. She couldn't read, and my grandmother grew from the inside out. She taught herself to be spiritual. Her own soul was her teacher. And the smile on her face was the light in her window that told others that there was a caring, sharing, very, very tough person inside. Yes, my grandmother was a fighter.

I think of Langston Hughes sometimes. He said in one of his poems, "Hold fast to dreams, For if dreams die, Life is a broken-winged bird, That cannot fly." I always felt my grandmother wanted to do so much more. But she never got a chance to fly.

Johnnie Powell

GOLDEN MOMENTS OF MY YOUTH

My neighborhood in New York was super special. It was an integrated neighborhood before that was acceptable. Black, white, Jews, Spanish, Catholic, and Protestant. All the elders were my fathers and mothers. I got encouragement from every elder I met. We had always to address them as "yes sir," "yes ma'am," and if we didn't they would threaten us, then tell our parents, and I'd get a whipping.

All of us kids walked a tightrope on my block. We were such nice kids. But when we left our block we transformed into the worst kids on the planet, fighting and stealing. But we would never, never, bother old people.

If there was a car chase with the police chasing someone from our own neighborhood, we kids would back away from playing football, baseball, or whatever street game it was, and let the car go by. Then jump right back on the street so the police car had to stop. The chased car would then turn into a special garage that only we in the neighborhood knew where it was and disappear there.

There were also special houses on the block you could disappear into if someone was chasing you that only those in the neighborhood knew about, and you never told anyone, even if your life depended on it. No one was a snitch. My block was a family.

I can still hear the sounds of the ice cream man, the milkman in the morning, the knife sharpener, the junk man, the numbers man. Everybody bet on the horses, and a $5 bet could bring you $250. There was a nightclub on the end of the block. Me and my friends knew when the chorus girls would be changing into their costumes. A hole was dug into the wall and we would watch them undress. But we made so much noise that the bouncer would come out and say he was going to call our parents. And that was that.

My block was a runway to high accomplishments. People began to leave the city for Long Island. For us kids it was a sad day. All that music, adventure, all those people. Those wonderful, wonderful times.

Johnnie Powell

MY GREENWICH VILLAGE

There is Greenwich Village, world famous, then there is my Greenwich Village. We used to call it the free four square miles on the planet earth, full of all kinds of people, famous and not famous, rich and poor, beautiful people. A place of profound magic. I remember Bob Dylan sitting at a sidewalk cafe, drinking. He wasn't famous then, but he was well known around the Village. So many talented people, all this knowledge and wisdom.

To me, there was an invisible fence around the Village. You knew when you ventured out of it; the language was different, people were deadly, serious, threatening, selfish. There were thieves, but if one of those thieves kissed you, you had better count your teeth. I never stayed away from the Village long. I would always run back.

In the Village we stuck together. Snowflakes are frail, but if enough of them stick together they can stop traffic. Individually, we are one drop, but together we are an ocean. The Village was a mighty ocean. Wow! For a moment, one long good moment, I found Shangri-La.

The artist, Matisse, said it bothered him all his life that he did not paint like everybody else. Greenwich Village painted life like no one else. It was a place that believed in kissing, where you cherished your solitude, slept alone under the stars, learned how to drive a stick shift, and said *Yes* if your instincts were strong, even if everyone around you disagreed; you could decide whether you wanted to be liked or admired; a place you could say *No* whenever you didn't want to do something. You could go so far away with God that you stopped being afraid of not coming back. But don't judge me by my past; I don't live there anymore.

Johnnie Powell

MOTOWN

Motown for me was the heartbeat. It influenced my life. I'd wake up in the morning singing and dancing, and say my prayers or do my meditation to some Motown sound. I'd see Jesus standing up on his throne popping his fingers and dancing with me. I'd tell this to my mom and she'd say, "Boy, you crazy!"

Stevie Wonder, Smokey Robinson: some Motown sound was always playing in the streets. The music was everywhere and all life had a rhythm. At the park where we played basketball we'd be dancing, listening to some Motown jam and playing supernatural ball. I loved being in the streets. Music, music, music!

Johnnie Powell

MRS. HOUGHTON

I was raised in New York City. School was exciting concerning sports, but I was terrible in class. I just couldn't get into English, math or science. School for me was sports, football and track. I graduated from high school with a Circle 65, meaning I just made it. But I got a scholarship to play football at a college in Garden City, Kansas, a thousand miles from home, where the people worked on farms and were like Neanderthals to me. They all seemed to be fifty years behind the times. There were Mennonites, Amish-looking people, people whose clothes looked like they were from the 1920s.

I loved the football program. We were two hundred guys from all over the country and we all bonded well. One day into my class for under-achievers comes this lady with silver hair, maybe sixty-years-old, with horn-rimmed glasses and tailored clothes. Her face was beautiful, motherly and happy. You knew she was not from Kansas. Her name was Mrs. Houghton. She began to speak about English and books. I thought she was from outer space. I'd never heard anybody speak about books and study like that before. When she spoke it was like the sun coming out on a gloomy day. My life changed that day.

Our class was all football players but Mrs. Houghton was in charge. She was the lion tamer and wise as a serpent. She made us all look deep into ourselves. Our language changed around her. She produced eagles. She made us all feel special. Smart or dumb, everybody became a golden child in her class. By the time I graduated two years later, I had read five hundred books of all kinds, in addition to those required for my studies.

Today, I never go to bed without learning something. A new word I didn't know, some historical fact. Something. That little lady made learning a pleasure. I love learning. Mrs. Houghton taught me, "He who is accompanied by noble thoughts is never alone." I don't play football anymore but I continually seek knowledge. Through reading and studying I have found a most delicious inner life. I like who I am. What an adventure books have brought me.

Johnnie Powell

FOOTBALL IN THE SNOW

Playing football in the snow in college in Kansas was an experience. You really had to psych yourself up in the locker room before running into the stadium. And you had to spend a lot of extra time warming up as it is so easy to break an arm or leg on a snowy day. But once the game started you turned into another person and didn't feel the cold.

When it came to snow we all loved playing a college from a warm climate, like California or Florida. They couldn't play in the cold. They'd be so busy trying to stay warm they'd fumble a shot and drop passes they'd usually catch. And they ran tentatively on snowy ground, with no power. You could see in their eyes that they didn't want to be on the field, which was like cement, frozen and hard. But we were accustomed to the weather, and I remember sliding all over the field with it snowing so hard you could hardly see what was in front of you. Sometimes the wind would blow so hard that if you kicked or passed the ball it would stay up in the air longer. I remember feeling invincible in the cold. Boy, I loved football.

Johnnie Powell

MIRACLE ON 59TH STREET

For a couple years I lived in Spanish Harlem in the days when there was a lot of tension between Black and Spanish gangs. I had an incredible apartment there in El Barrio, but every day I had to be ready for a fight if one did happen. I always carried an ice pick and a gun, and never never never went anywhere without those weapons. And at the end of the day when I got off the Iron Horse (as the subway was known) I was always prepared for war.

Until one day something strange happened. I left my apartment without my weapons and thought nothing of it. As I got off the subway at 59th Street, who do I see coming toward me but my ex-wife, who got all the gold in our divorce and I got the shaft. I hadn't seen her in ten years. As we meet I see daggers in her eyes, and for a moment something in me snapped, and I reached for my weapons. They weren't there! Wow! How could I have left home without them? Then I realized that a great tragedy had just been avoided and that God must have foreseen this moment. After that I moved from El Barrio, New York, to Long Island, and never carried weapons of any kind ever again.

Johnnie Powell

1968

What a Year! I got out of the military that April and went to California. To San Francisco, Haight-Ashbury. Wow! Beautiful people everywhere. Lots of sex, drugs, and rock n' roll. The Grateful Dead had a house where everyone was invited to come in and smoke a joint. Incredible clothes, flower power, psychedelic music, hippies. I had this huge Afro, bell bottoms, high heel shoes, a bandana, and always a $20 bag of marijuana. The song was, "If you're going to San Francisco / Be sure to wear some flowers in your hair . . ."

In 1968, all kinds of people from every level of life wanted change in this country: The Anti-War movement, the Civil Rights Movement... People were hoping for revolutionary change, and it was happening already in the Peoples' Republic of Berkeley. Those were high times and not because of "Lucy in the Sky with Diamonds." The great question at the time wasn't "Who is going to let me?" It was "Who is going to stop me?" I remember seeing a sign somewhere that said, "If you think education is expensive, try ignorance."

But the quotation I remember most was from Martin Luther King Jr., when he said, "Our lives begin to end the day we become silent about things that matter." I left the Bay Area a year later, realizing that just as coal is transformed into diamonds because of intense pressure, so too it's only through our challenges that we can change.

Johnnie Powell

STARS CAN'T SHINE WITHOUT DARKNESS

Everyone you meet is fighting a battle you know nothing about. So be kind, always. I had a college friend named Tony. I couldn't stand him. We hated each other, or so I thought. We both had great big egos, were both very popular in school, had the finest of clothes and plenty of girlfriends. One day, maybe five years after college, I saw him coming down the street toward me. This hatred came upon me from our school days. He tried to say hello and be friendly, but I wasn't having it. My heart was like arctic ice towards him and I kept going.

Some weeks later I ran into another college buddy and we began talking about the old days. Then he says to me, "Did you hear about Tony?" He told me how Tony had gone to jail on some minor charge and that he had been raped. How he had gotten out just a couple of weeks ago and had barely gone home and he committed suicide. And I thought about my attitude and actions toward him. Maybe, just maybe, my hard-heartedness towards him had pushed him over the edge. I cried and cried and cried. I made up my mind from that moment on that my life would be a statement of love and compassion, and where it wasn't I would make it so.

This is my letter to the world that never wrote to me. Never, never, never underestimate the power of a touch, a smile, a kind word, a listening ear, an honest compliment or the smallest act of caring. All have the power and potential to turn a life around. Tony, I will never forget you. Where I go, you go.

Johnnie Powell

HOPE

Those who wish to sing always find a song. Most of the important things in the world have been accomplished by people who kept on trying when there seemed to be no hope at all. Sometimes, when I look at what is happening to our country—the economy, the mental illness on the streets, the floods, storms, the devastating death of birds, fishes, people out of work, the millions on food stamps—I could go on and on—it seems so hopeless!!

Then, I go and sit with God and look on the earth and I am steeled for combat. I realize that God gives nothing to those who keep their arms crossed and that freedom always entails danger. Hope is faith holding out its hand in the dark. Hope never abandons us; we abandon it. We have all been in the gutter of life sometimes. But some of us, even there, are looking up at the stars. I've heard it said that man can live about forty days without food, about three days without water, about eight minutes without air. But only seconds without hope.

When we say a situation or person is without hope, we are slamming the door in the face of God. What oxygen is to the lungs, such is hope to the meaning of life. "Hope is the thing with feathers, that perches in the soul, and sings the tune without words and never, never stops at all." Emily Dickinson said that. May we have enough happiness to make us sweet, enough trials to make us strong, enough sorrow to keep us human, and enough hope to make us happy.

Taumstar

Taumstar was born in Utah, into a large family. She often recalls her complicated relationship with her father, whom she loved and admired, but he also made her aware of her "shortcomings." She joined Safe Place Writing Circle in July, 2014, unsure of herself as a poet. The prompt that day was, "Count Your Blessings," with the idea that giving thanks can be any day of the year, not just the last Thursday in November. Taumstar was delighted by the concept and wrote "Thanksgiving on Friday?," a celebration of that day, her first experience with Safe Place. She's rarely missed a class since.

Early on, she shared that she had "made a deal" with her voices to leave her alone during her Safe Place time so that she could focus and participate better. The deal seems to have gone great, and her participation is always lively and focused. She has a natural affinity for poetry, and the ability to say a lot with a few words. Her writing is bold and original, and often playful as she confronts her own life struggles and beliefs, often with wonderful leaps from one idea to another to find connections between seemingly disparate concepts.

Taumstar's enjoyment and appreciation of life is infectious, as is her laugh. Her view of the world is deeply spiritual without being overtly religious, and infused with an appreciation for eastern philosophy. Within the group she is both warmly supportive of others and a careful listener, someone who's not afraid to say what she thinks or ask a question.

I don't want it all!
If I have it all, then what do you have?

Taumstar

REGRETS?

Should've. Could've. Would've. Didn't.

There was a time
when touched in the head was off limits.
In my youth, I visited a nursing home.
A place where elder people were cared for.
To show respect, I quietly listened while each elder
expressed their view. Elder ladies.
I was supposed to refer to them as "ma'am"
and to answer "yes ma'am" was enough.

They talked about the good old days,
their young days. The ability to speak
was strained, the volume soft.
The lips moved somewhat.
There were also times when suddenly
they'd just forget, their thought no more.

Aging: rest and naps are on the schedule
more often, suggesting social life
will be unfolding at a slow rate.
But who keeps a tally of regrets? All those memories
of youth and past discussions about should have,
could have, would have, and didn't.

What a memory is, is.
Regrets? They don't change anything.

Taumstar

FINDING MY VOICE

Be Quiet and Listen.

In my head are many voices,
so which one, or who in particular
should I listen to?
Finding my voice in my voices . . . .
But they are *all* mine . . .

What would you like to converse about?

My voices keep me company.
We have lengthy discussions,
not always real useful
other than I am not alone.
A voice will speak to remind me.
You are not alone. Be grateful.

Thank you, I say. I am.

The voice is not the challenge.
For me, choosing
the correct words for the voice to speak
and be heard is the challenge.

Taumstar

FUNNY

It is not funny.
It is too,
just a playful little pinch,
an itty-bitty crime . . .
It is not funny.
It is too.

When frustration
takes your breath, and you lose
your voice, you even change color.
It isn't funny.
It is too.

Your volume goes up,
being coherent goes down.
Your words come out fast,
their meaning not clear.
It isn't funny.
It is too.

Rational behavior is preferred.
Perception. Protocol. Performance.
Permission and acceptability.
May I be included?

Funny doesn't always mean
to laugh. It can mean unfamiliar, even strange.
But when funny brings a smile, we all heal.

Taumstar

CRY AND TRANSFORM

5 AM.
Walk briskly.   Will rain.
The ego is anxious.
The ego wants no change.
But change has already occurred—
an exercise in love,
            picking up and going forward.

At the same time, sadness.
Feel older. Accomplishments?
Not everyone gets to accomplish much.
Gratitude.
            Thanksgiving.
Going to a back and spine doctor—
            they are not so quick to prescribe.
Started doing yoga, again.
No longer able to sweep, prune, saw, hammer.   No heavy lifting.

Learn / unlearn.
No longer get to drive.
Must think about
                mobility = long term ability.
The little stuff more hard . . .
                Cry and transform.

Taumstar

SHADOWS

What makes a shadow?
The light from behind.

sun in the morning
sun in the afternoon
moon in the evening
moon in the morning twilight.

I am thinking a shadow has two parts,
plus its edge. The light from behind
defines the edge of the shadow while
the light from the front defines
yet another edge of the same shadow.

Each day begins in the east
at the horizon of dawn.
Each day the sun moves across the sky.
Each day ends with the sun slipping
out of sight to the west.

The moon follows the same pattern.
Every day. Every night.

I like shadows. I do shadow yoga.
I like the quiet silence of shadows.
Shadows are always in step and in form.
My yoga shadow can hear all my thoughts
and commands, and translate them into
movement, all without verbal prompting.

The breath cycle is the same.
My self and all of my shadows
move in graceful motion together.

The edge. The edges.
Without the sun and moon for light,
and for contrast, I would be very alone.
There would be no shadow.

The white light leaves no edge.
The white light leaves no shadow.

Taumstar

GETTING OLDER

Is Alzheimer's isolated
to older people? I am thinking . . .
maybe I can graduate
        from mental illness
        to Alzheimer's
just by living longer.

No need to know so much
about . . . What?

Okay. Without prescriptions
I'm clear headed, calm, and quiet. Do yoga.
With prescriptions I'm lethargic,
with total brain-fog.

As I get older I ask,
what do I know that will change?
An idea appears. But is it inside out?
Upside down? Is it a lie?

Oh God! It is gone.
Bleep!

Taumstar

LOVE

I am sure that I will learn
how to love without prejudice.
I realize to love is the duty
of each one to the other.

There is no choice about love.
It is the command.

I like Jesus best.
He is my one brother
who never sexually assaulted me.

I do have a choice who I like.
Love everyone is the command.
Learning how it all turns out
will be an adventure.

Taumstar

THANKSGIVING ON FRIDAY?

Count my blessings?
Gratitude list?

Okay.

Today is Friday
The summer temperature of 76 degrees is great.
Safe Place. A Refuge.

Thanksgiving is any time and all the time.
Quiet, calm, present.

I *do* feel something.
I *am* grateful.
Friday, and today *is* Thanksgiving.

Taumstar

TOUGH RELATIONSHIPS

Daddy.
The house that Jack built.
King Midas.
Captain Hook.
The robber on the cross.
Captain Jack Sparrow.
The lion and the house.
If it were not for their extreme behavior
these would not be mentioned.
Even Jesus Christ is best known
for the crucifixion
and the resurrection.

Taumstar

WHAT DO I KNOW?

I know at my house
there lives an Australian Shepherd,
weighing about 75 pounds, tri-colored
black, brown and white
and with a nub for a tail.
In the same house there are two green birds,
both girls; one is named Rio,
Jackie is the other. Both birds bite.
Very pretty to look at but
don't get too close.

The cat that lives here is a Calico,
about nine years old, and with large thumbs
on both front feet making them very large.
This cat will tell you what she knows.

There are two peeps that also hang out
here at my house,
large and small, male and female.
They each do this and that,
service and maintenance
so that harmony may prevail.

At 4 AM the day begins, alarm sounds off.
Peeps begin moving, slow at first.
Still dark, they can't see, but it's morning,
time to get up, get dressed,
eat a light breakfast and drink something hot.
Say thank you, the sun will soon be up.

This is what I know.

Taumstar

MIRROR

When I look, I stay
and study.
I familiarize my eyes.
I see the reflection
and try to remember.
Is everything the same?
Has the landscape changed?

At a much younger age,
the map of life's journey
shows skin still smooth
with not much wear.
How uninteresting!

A question:
What makes a wrinkle?
And why does a smile have so many wrinkles?
even a baby's smile . . .
Are wrinkles to be limited
to the aging only?
If so, how uninteresting.

Angel Ybarra

Angel grew up in Spokane, and other parts of Washington. Of mixed descent, with a Mexican father and German-American mother, Angel is the oldest of three girls. Her childhood was chaotic, and often unsafe, due mainly to her mother's drinking and mental illness, with frequent moves and changes of school. Angel's teen years were mostly spent in foster care and group homes for runaways. Her past still haunts her, and flashbacks of past traumas sometimes leave her wishing she could erase her memory.

Discovering herself as an artist has been, and continues to be, a vital part of her recovery and making peace with the past. She enjoys many different art forms, and has taken numerous visual art classes, as well as writing, and, more recently, dance. She also trained as a yoga teacher, and sometimes leads yoga classes at the Café.

It is writing that sustains Angel from day to day. She's a storyteller, a quality that shows in all her writing. She carries a notebook everywhere she goes, and is always engaged in writing and rewriting her life story in some form or other, often revisiting the same story or life event but in new ways, from a different vantage point. Her complicated relationship with her mother is at the center of much of her writing, including the pieces featured here, which are also excerpts of a memoir in progress.

Angel first came to Safe Place over three years ago. Sometimes she's gone for a while, usually to try her hand at something new in another class. Then she's back again, notebook in hand, hungry for new prompts and happy to be back in the group.

Anything is possible. I am living proof.

Angel Ybarra

EYES ON FIRE

It's not an everyday occurrence that cops are trying to get your mother from out underneath the deck of the house. The men in blue try to coax her out. They tell her the rats are going to get her. Nothing surprises me anymore with her. It's just a matter of when and how.

She came home shortly after midnight. I'm on the phone, and my sisters are sound asleep when she storms through the front door with fire in her eyes. Clearly, this is not going to be a peaceful night. Her Maybelline Mascara smeared around her eyes and her gritted teeth never fail to set the tone: danger. And already the war within her has put many battle scars on my heart.

I watch her swagger as she still holds onto the doorknob. Her eyes are like daggers. "You!" she slurs, with her finger pointed straight at me. I immediately hang up the phone and head straight for my room, which is in the basement. But tonight, I leave my door slightly ajar and keep the light off. My pink clock glows 12:23 AM. My dad should be home at any time. I don't know how he does it, working two jobs to cover all the bad checks Mother's written. How many times has she spent the rent check buying drinks for the bar? But that's the way she is, the center of every situation; the life of the party. To everyone else she can do no wrong, and like the sun, people gravitate towards her.

The moon looks full tonight. It dangles there, peering in on me through my window. It's a typical basement window, small and narrow, that I recently discovered I could climb out of after sneaking my boyfriend in. Dad came home early that day, so to cover my tracks I climbed out with Allen. Right now the house is eerily quiet. Maybe Mom's actually going to pass out early tonight. I sit up, thinking about Allen and the last time we kissed. That was behind the high school. I'm only fourteen and I still can't believe a junior is interested in me. Doesn't he know I am not real liked by most kids? I feel out of his league.

A loud thump above snaps me out of my reverie. I hear Michael Jackson's song, "Thriller," way loud. Tonight the liquid is bringing out Mom's dancing talents. She is a force to be reckoned with. A jack-of-all-trades and a dancer of all sorts: ballet, modern jazz, tap—even go-go. I hear her upstairs, dancing all over the living room. I can almost see her twirls, and I'm certain she's wearing her Michael Jackson black hat to fit the occasion.

The music stops, and her feet patter across the floor to her room directly above me. Maybe this time she will just go to sleep? I gaze back up at the moon and wonder if I could walk away from all this, permanently. I remember a time when I was younger. I was sitting in the back seat of Dad's car, and we'd just left the river. Music was blaring on the car radio, and Mom was crazy drunk, hanging out the window and howling like a dog. She even climbed out, with Dad trying to stop her and still trying to drive. I remember staring out the window and imagined myself jumping out of the car and running straight for the woods, never looking back. I imagined myself running and running into nothingness.

Now I hear a noise. It sounds like it's coming from the top of the stairs that connect my room directly to the kitchen. I think, maybe it's the kittens playing up there. I stare at the crack of light along the side of my door and listen intently. Nothing. My eyes wander back to the moon at the window. I'm not hearing anything above me any more, and am certain she has gone to bed this time. But now there's that peculiar sound again, from the top of the stairwell. I keep hearing it. I'm staring at the slit of light at my door not understanding why but sensing trouble. That's why I keep the door ajar. Knowing my mother, I'm always expecting something to happen.

I hear her running across the living room. She's screaming something. I can tell she's made it to my sister's room. I'm leaning on my elbows, still peering at that slit of light. Time is moving slowly. I sit up, and it feels like my feet take forever to plant on the ground. My eyes are glued to that slit of light. Somehow, the light looks different and I don't know why. My feet feel like bricks with each step I take. I reach for the doorknob. But I hesitate. What am I going to find? My mother's yelling is frantic. Suddenly, my door seems to be about twenty feet tall. It's almost too heavy to open.

At first glance I don't see anything unusual. But when I turn toward the stairwell I see flames crawling up the wall, and curling higher. For a moment it's like the devil glaring down, screaming, "Look! Look what you made me do you little bitch!" The fire has not yet entirely engulfed the whole stairwell. There isn't much time. I think about the window in my room. But if I climb out the window the whole house is going to go up in flames. I begin climbing the stairs like a warrior prepared for war.

Angel Ybarra

STAIRWAY TO HEAVEN

I'd just hit my teens. It was late summer when the heat was thick. I found myself bored and restless, wanting something to do. Music has always been my thing when all else fails. Mom and Dad were not home. Dad was working and who knew where Mama was. I turned on the stereo, you know, that 80s style with the glass door and tall speakers. Mom and Dad didn't have much money so theirs wasn't the biggest one on the block but it did its job. I opened the door, turned the power button on, and went through the static to find my favorite rock stations. Those days, the popular music was Aerosmith, Def Leppard, Guns N' Roses. AC/DC was my favorite band although I did like me some Lita Ford too.

I saw a few cassette tapes sitting on the lower deck of the stereo where records are stored. I'm not sure what happened to all of Mom's and Dad's records; maybe they pawned them, who knows. I did notice this white cassette tape that stood out from a few others. It read *Led Zeppelin IV.* I popped it in and the first song I heard was "Black Dog." My ears really enjoyed it. Something about the voice caught my attention. Later I realized it was Robert Plant's voice. I went through the whole cassette, but before getting to the B-side, I absolutely fell in love with the last song on the A-side: Good ol' "Stairway to Heaven." A very beautiful song. What I couldn't understand was how I could like Mama's music. Kids don't like their parent's music, or do they? Just the day before, Mama had come home smelling of booze with that same old mascara run around her eyes. She turned on the stereo blaring it as loud as it could go, and began dancing all around the house. That was my mama, always getting her groove on.

I realized that Mama probably picked up that cassette somewhere while partying. I decided to keep the tape, certain she wouldn't ever notice it missing. I planned on blaring it in my boombox as much as I could. This was going to be my little secret: teenage girl steals Mom's

Led Zeppelin cassette and hides it away so no one would know she liked her mom's music. Then, one day, walking home from school, a peculiar thing happened. I saw this boy with long brown hair walking too. I'd seen him around school. I noticed he was wearing a black t-shirt and as I got closer I saw that it read "Led Zeppelin." I couldn't believe it! My secret band that I'd fallen in love with was a band that many people loved. All I can say is Mama knows how to party and get down with rock 'n roll! Yay Mama!

Angel Ybarra

BEAUTY QUEEN

She was more like a beauty queen from a movie scene . . .
from "Billie Jean" —Michael Jackson

I was eight-years-old when Michael Jackson made yet another mark on the world. He'd already entered into every household with access to MTV, which was fairly new at the time in the early 1980s. In our home it was a tradition to watch the *Thriller* video every night at 5 o'clock sharp, and Friday night was music and dancing night with the family. Mom and Dad would play their records or sometimes their 8-tracks, but whenever they popped in "Billie Jean," it was time for Mama to put on her black dancing hat, like the one Michael Jackson wore.

See, Mama was a performer. She used to dance on Broadway—ballet, tap, and jazz—Mama did it all. On Friday nights, the three of us girls would climb up on the couch, our feet dangling, as Dad introduced Mama, and the living room became her stage. Those were the fun times growing up. Because, in my house, when things were good they were really good, and when they were bad, they were bad.

On this particular night everything was perfect. Dad was smiling and my sisters were giddy with excitement. I couldn't wait for Mama's performance to start. It was always so much fun to watch her quick moves to the beat, with all her twirls mixed up with both ballet and jazz. With her black hat tipped the same way Michael Jackson tipped his, she waited for the record to start. We clapped our hands with anticipation, and then the living room went silent for a moment with only the crisp static sound of the record player. And then she was dancing and twirling on our hearts. Like the song goes, "She was more like a beauty queen from a movie scene." She's the one who dances on the floor leaving smiles on our faces. Mama was good at dancing and twirling on our hearts. We never were tired of her performance, especially when she did Michael Jackson's famous move, the Moonwalk. We were her crowd screaming and shouting for more. Nothing else mattered on Friday nights. I never wanted them to end.

It would take me many years to understand Mama. She had a pain deep within her, a beautiful blonde with so many talents. I would not know the extent of her illness and her afflictions for some time. Eventually, her torment left her walking off the stage never to return. We prayed for her to come back and perform again for us. But it was too late. There wasn't anything we could do for her. She was never coming back.

I grew up, and some years later my own illness would turn out to be the same as hers. Everything began to make sense. I suddenly had a new perspective of what life was like for Mama. I will never fully understand the desecration she bestowed upon me. I only learned that things don't look as they appear, and at the same time someone who deals with mental illness and addiction is sometimes the most talented, caring, and loving person you can ever come across. A beauty queen from a movie scene is only half of Mama's story.

Angel Ybarra

ANTS IN YOUR PANTS

I watch the trail of fat bubbly red ants bustle in and out of the hole beneath me. My little hands grip onto the wooden fence. My feet rest on the lower part of the fence holding me up as my chin rests on the top. I've done this time and time before. My dad always says, "Watch out for those big red ants, they hurt when they bite." When he was a child he fell into a nest in Glendale, Arizona, where he was born and raised. My dad really knows the meaning of ants in your pants. His story resonated with me so much so that I became cautious, I did not want to experience the same thing. For me, this was my first revelation of fear, although it never stopped me from being curious about ants.

I hang on tightly to the fence, watching the ants go about their little lives in this sweltering heat. The air is thick, like a fever I had the year before. The hallucinations I had then were like mirages out on the desolate flat land, which slowly disappeared whenever I tried getting closer. The long walks with my dad were the same. My mouth would be cracked and dried, so thirsty for some water. Up ahead I'd see what I thought to be water, but no matter how far we walked we never reached it.

Now, in the distance, saguaros stand tall, with beautiful majestic mountains along the horizon. I can smell the rain from the night before, and sweet wet sage permeates the air. A light sultry wind stirs up the dusty and lonely land. I look back down at the ants. The sun caresses my cheeks. I notice the trail of ants has moved to a post nearer to my foot that is holding me up. I hurry to move farther down away from their travels. I am captivated by their existence. In a tree across the way, I hear the locusts' echoes, their cries and their songs of love as they peal out of the tree. Locusts were the ones to harvest love in my child's heart. On my long walks with my dad, we would catch them and cup them in our hands, then set them free to the skies, my brown eyes watching in amazement as they flew away.

Behind me my dad is pushing the mower. I turn to watch him. He's wearing his sombrero. He doesn't see me watching. The grass is as tall as me. Most of the mower's blades are a crispy brown. My dad looks so strong. He is the greatest man on this earth, and he makes me laugh. Whenever I ask him what's for dinner he always replies, "Oh, the usual, grasshoppers, spiders, and cockroaches." And each time I look in the pan just to be sure. But he never mentions those big, fat, red ants.

Angel Ybarra

THE NARROW WAY

The hallway is mayhem filled with cops, medics and on-looking neighbors. All I can hear is my frantic voice screaming. Everything else fades in and out. I hear the police say something, I'm not sure what. Everything else is a blur, like a movie reel, with each scene blinking in and out of view.

All I remember is a large knife grazing across my throat. I am on my knees, and blood is dripping onto the kitchen floor. I'm screaming. But why am I painting my hands in the blood? Have I gone insane? I smear blood all over my face. Nothing is making sense, and my world is spinning out of control. I think I hear Steven's voice at the end of the hallway, and I scream out his name in desperation. The only reply is the men in blue, informing me I am under arrest: "Ma'am, you have the right to remain silent." And I fade away.

When I open my eyes there is a bright light above me. I hear someone say, "She has had a lot to drink and her boyfriend stated she swallowed a bunch of pills." I still don't understand. Why is this happening? I pray that it's all a nightmare and I will wake up soon. Then I fade again . . . .

This time my eyes open to an empty room. I am a little more alert but don't feel well. I see an officer sitting outside the door. He is filling out paperwork. I realize I'm going to jail. My state of mind switches, and I shut down. Survival mode. I need to accept my fate. I think to myself, I must call home. I know it's earlier there than here, but also know my mother will answer the phone. I see the phone on the wall beside me and reach for it. I dial the number. The phone rings twice and Mom picks up.

"Mom!" I say desperately, "I am in trouble. I have done it this time."

"What happened?" she asks with concern in her voice. But her voice also sounds lagged. I know it's the effects of the Methadone.

"I don't know, Mom. Steven and I were fighting and after that everything went crazy. We had a lot to drink . . . but I don't understand how it led to this . . . Mom, I am in so much trouble, Mom! I lost it!" The cop came in. It was time for me to hang up. "Mom, I have to go now. I will call you when I get to booking, okay?"

I barely comprehend the ride to the station. Next thing I know they are taking my fingerprints. Someone's telling me to look to one side. I hear a camera then see a flash of light. Now it's time for my one phone call from jail. The phones are all lined up against the wall, a familiar sight. I get connected through to my mom and we talk for a while. My mind races. Mom is telling me something about her legs, but I am unable to really comprehend what she is saying. Then the phone goes dead and my heart sinks like a ship going under.

The cell door echoes shut, and I stare at the cemented floor where a green mattress lays. They've put me on suicide watch. My heart hurts. I feel so alone, and my soul cries out, wishing for this to all go away. I lie on the mattress and curl into a ball. I'm cold with no blanket and no socks. I am dressed in a musty blue jumpsuit made for a man, and it smells like sweat. It's protocol to put anyone under suicide watch in a jumpsuit so they can easily be identified. I'm familiar with the smell, and know it never goes away, no matter how many times they're washed. I feel like I am in a dungeon, lying under a dim light that never shuts off. Briefly, I fall asleep, and wake up feeling sicker than a dog, my eyes heavy as I try to open them. As the room comes into focus I find myself staring directly under the toilet, which is caked with piss and shit and has dried toilet paper stuck to it. I am desperately cold. It takes everything in me to sit up so that I can reach myself up to the window of my cell door. I need to ask for more toilet paper.

I hear a clanging of keys. My mind plays tricks on me, and it seems there is a giant hole in the middle of my cell. The cell door grows farther and farther away from me, and my head feels light. The floor has opened up to a glowing fire pit. Is this my hell on earth? I have to get to the door. It fades in and out of view. I focus on the small caged square. Once again I hear the clanging of keys. My voice cracks, "Excuse me officer, can I please have some toilet paper?" He comes to the door. "Don't you have any?" He looks through the window to check, and when he doesn't see any he brings a roll and slides it through the slot, then slams it shut. I take out the other roll I had hidden in my jumpsuit and unravel it to wrap some around my feet like slippers, and use the new roll to tuck under my head like a pillow. I try to fall asleep.

For the next three days I try calling home, but cannot get through. On the third day, I call one of my sisters and am connected right away. But the relief I feel is only temporary. The first words my sister utters are that our mom has passed away. I cannot believe what my ears are hearing, and for a moment I am frozen in time, in denial of her words. Then I fall to my knees screaming, "NO!" My voice echoes through the jail and I'm surrounded by the men in blue. Time moves in slow motion, my legs like jelly dragging underneath me. I am desperate not to be taken back into my cell. But I'm carried, cops holding me under each arm. I look back to see faces peering out of their cell windows, and a voice calls out, "You're in my prayers!" An old man makes eye contact and I see sadness in his eyes. "I will pray for you," he says. For a moment I feel the compassion of all the other inmates, but the men in blue are cold as the door slams behind me.

I spent the next six months in this desolate place. My lawyer told me I could be put away for twelve years. Some days went by fast, other days the time felt like the minutes were hours. I kept busy by drawing and writing. I stayed to myself most of the time. Other days I laughed hysterically with the other inmates. Then I'd go numb. It was my way of coping. I still hadn't cried a whole lot over my mother's death. There is no room to cry in a place like jail. It's a dark place to be. A lot of women are angry, some are evil, others lost and hurting. Most of the women are drug-addicted like myself, living in violence and chaos. But AA Meetings were held every Thursday, and I attended every week. AA was my life-line for hope for my future. I was tired of living my life in turmoil. The meetings fed me almost like a drug fix. The two ladies who held those meetings became part of my life, even after I was released from jail. Still, AA didn't become my light at the end of the tunnel for a while. My time in jail did change me. I had so much to process.

I stumbled many times after this chapter in my life. Eventually I got it together after putting myself through more trials and tribulations. It was those experiences that finally woke me up. I learned I was still running from myself. Sometimes we have to feel the pain of our darkness before we can see our own worth. It takes what it takes. We have a saying in the twelve-step programs, "When the pain gets great enough then we will do something about it." I have learned to live one day at a time. I am not responsible for the bad things that were done to me but I am responsible for my recovery. I know I never have to live the way I was living ever again. It's my choice, and today I choose to love myself first. Without that I have nothing.

II

Other Voices

Diana Balgaard

ODE TO JAMIE

Shingles, gray, worn and tattered
adorned the old house. Trees and shrubs
dotted the yard, ignored, unkempt.

Cloaked in darkness behind a metal fence
this property was out of step with the surrounding
neighborhood of manicured lawns
and filled my heart with sadness,
as my mind went to another time,
the old houses thrumming with hippie life
and you, Jamie, my love.

A time of fun and freedom, the only world
we knew at the time, and thought
(or at least I thought) it would go on
forever. Skinny dipping
in the old rock quarry and Cranberry Lake,
hidden in the woods,
until caught by a Park Ranger.
You and I immersed in love,
an ungrounded existence.

Then the sky fell.
"I'm going to Vietnam," you said.
"We will go different directions, you and I."
My whole body melted into nothing,
my whole body an avalanche of tears.
You went away then, to the afterlife.
My greatest love, you, Jamie, you were
an avatar to me, teaching me
what the world was supposed to be
and what we hoped it would become.

Diana Balgaard

BEAUTY PAGEANT BABY

How does your childhood feel?
Bred to be a Beauty, queen, diva;
an expensive ornament. You think
fame and glory will last forever.
Beauty spas, endured with pacifiers,
"Sit still Now" so you are the best
meal ticket ever. No time to play.
No time to feel your own laughter
or pain. Mom gives you a pill
to keep you perfect. Now, don't
get too rowdy, or the storm
will send you lightning.

Shelby Smith

ROLL WITH IT

Live alone if at all possible.
Live alone and face yourself.
Find out exactly who you are.

Sleep on clean cotton sheets.
Organic cotton.
Buy yourself four bed pillows
to support your comfort.

Allow comfort.
Shower before bed and
sleep like a baby.

Look forward to dreams.
Enjoy the show:
it's your production,
filled with your creations.

Do yoga whenever you want.
Make sure you have a special place.

Learn to accept yourself.
Can you be as loving and kind
to who you are as you can
to the people you love and admire?

Learn to roll.
Remember rolling down the grassy slopes.
Remember somersaults.
Remember that roundy feeling that makes you smile.

Find rivers. Find rivers
full of river rocks that are worn smooth.
Drive to beaches.
Find the inlets and the sounds and
the haystack rocks standing in the surf like castles.

Find out about bees.
Follow a bee if you can.
Watch bees if you can.

Imagine what the world might look
like if you had five eyes, one on top of your head.
Imagine you're a tree.
Feel your roots.
Make leaves and many blossoms.

Dance with the spirit of the air.
Dream of mountains and
temperature and
moving your legs and opening and closing
your mouth, and sound.

Remember how trees
in the mountains
and elsewhere
make cathedrals
with their geometry.

Breathe and believe
in what you experience
in creation.

Allow yourself to cry.
Allow yourself to remember

that the odds of creation are 50 billion to
50 billion and one.

Roll with that one
that has made everything possible.

Repeat as needed.
Share. Enjoy.

Cathy Scott

MOUNTAIN

This mountain is so high! How did I end up here? How, on God's green earth, did I ever expect myself . . . *me* . . . chubby, overweight, mentally challenged *me* . . . how, *why*, did I ever think I could manage this . . . this MOUNTAIN!!!???

One step forward. I *did* go forward, didn't I? Yep . . . a step forward . . . and a step up . . . Oops! Okaaayy . . . Steady as we go. Up . . . up . . . Oh shit! Down. Back at the bottom. I need help. Oh, heellppp!! Anybody out there? Geez, leave it to me to pick the one morning when the entire world slept in! Help!! Louder!!! *Help*!!!!!!

Wait! Listen . . . . a faint whispering . . . a breeze? The air seems lighter. I see. I can see a little better. Just a little better . . . and a little higher. I feel a little lighter on my feet. A Hand, a strong and gentle Hand is on me, lifting me, gently lifting me. The top is getting closer . . . closer . . . The mountain? It really isn't a mountain, after all. Just bushes and steps, and not so very steep, the top just a gentle, loving nudge away.

Allen Taylor

A THOUSAND SHADOWS AND ONLY ONE BODY

Shadows
and shadows among shadows.
Your eyes see only one
but often not the same.

Shadows.
We all have a shadow, and
some mingle among shadows.
But I own one too many.

Shadows.
My original wakes with me,
follows me all day,
and goes to bed when I do.
But very rarely does this other one
venture out.

Shadows.
They share one body
but the image is always changing.

Shadows
Like the annoying squawking ticket to
the migraine city-spoiled child.

I decide which to wear.

Every third Saturday of
the month; or
every time Pride Fest is here
it becomes a war of who, and what.

Shadows.
Even Halloween is a hard time.
Choosing?
Money wasted on one,
only to waste more for the other.

Shadows.
The Countess is the most
expensive, and often favored,
but such a picky little bitch
she complains if a fur coat has a zipper!

Shadows
and shadows among shadows:
safer than possession for those
who can't afford an exorcist.

Thank God a photo studio
can fit us all,
or I'd have to disown a hundred or more.

Dana Nelson Dudley

AUTUMN MEMORIES

The last really good memory I have
of my brothers is walking on Capitol Hill
on a street with huge maples
that had huge leaves, many of which
had fallen all over the streets and sidewalks,
the three of us like little kids,
because to walk was to kick.
You had to kick the leaves to walk.

It reminded me of us as kids
on vacation in California—
or was it the Southwest?
—playing *Bonanza*.
We three were as one. The three sons,
like the Three Musketeers, or the Three Stooges,
or the sitcom, *My Three Sons*.

Or another occasion, a sober one,
our dad had had a stroke.
We all flew up for a long weekend visit
in the midst of a glorious autumn.
Dad seemed to be alright,
but all of us were wondering . . .
Meanwhile, we had the gift of sharing
a wonderful autumn evening.

Like a dream it is to me now,
the three of us bound by a strange love.
Our mother said it well:
"Nowhere have I ever seen
three men so unusually alike
and yet so totally different."

Dana Nelson Dudley

FREMONT BRIDGE

I would love to jump off
the little, low Fremont Bridge,
with its paint fairly fresh still.
I love its pigeons,
those gentle birds with iridescent
necks and friendly coos.
Nice bright white pigeon turds
smear the bridge's pavement
and foot tracks of heedless pedestrians.
When I ride the bus I love to see
the blue and orange girders of the bridge
go up, then down to freedom and
that great joy called "moving on."

HarloweRayne E. Thunderword-Cohen

RAPTURE

Clad in an itchy has-been choir robe and well worn comfy jeans, I'm pacing back and forth, back and forth like a boxer about to enter the ring to fight The Battle of My Life! I'm tense, nervous as all get-out! Bending down at the the waist, I try to focus and gather myself in.

I squeeze my eyes shut. Why am I so damn nervous? Geez, I've fantasized and imagined this moment. I hear the roar of the crowd, the frenetic footfalls of folks darting to and fro, the arranging of chairs and their occupants. The joint is "Call the fire marshal!" packed, with warm antsy bodies vibrating with anticipation. Now is not the time to back out! The man gives me the "get ready" cue, the music begins, and I begin bouncing lightly on my feet ready to do this thing.

The signal is given, and like Seabiscuit I'm off . . . skip-running down the linoleum aisle, deep into the semi-darkened sanctuary, past the ushers. I hit the stage. Briefly I'm still. Standing before the crowd . . . What the hell do I do next? My darting eyes quickly lock onto those of the choir conductor; she, sensing my angst, gives me discreet signals to guide me safely out of the dry dock of stagefright, and I began to move. It's on now! Eyes on the conductor and the lighting person, and I'm twirling, spinning, gliding my way into *that* place. Suddenly, it's just me, the center of attention, when, lifting my eyes upwards I spot it. An eight-foot high cross of sprayed metallic gold. It draws my soul toward it, hypnotized.

Feels like flying, as round and around I twirl, not even dizzy. I'm free. I'm floating, heart pounding, can't breath, the energy of the dance has me tightly cinched deep within its arms and I'm fighting the urge to just let go, surrender to the seductive allure of this dance, but I can't. I'm afraid to let go, to lose control in front of all these people. I run around the room, joyously encircle the crowd with an elated energy that can no longer be contained. Then the music stops and the applause begins, folks on their feet, cheering, clapping . . . And I can finally exhale, and take a bow.

III

Featured Writers

Bang Nguyen

Bang's family was the first Vietnamese refugee family to arrive in Seattle at the end of the Vietnam War. Bang was four years old. His childhood in Seattle was mostly secure and largely uneventful, and Bang did well in school and started what looked like a promising future in the corporate world. Not so. As Bang says in his writing, he "fell off the corporate ladder," and many other problems followed.

Central to the new life he is building for himself now is his role as an activist in the struggle to end homelessness, and as an advocate for affordable housing as a human right. His reclaiming of himself also includes more fully embracing his Vietnamese heritage and language, and he often brings elements of these into his writing.

He joined Safe Place with a certain confidence in his ability to write and express himself creatively, while also acknowledging that he was extremely "rusty" in both areas. Eager to get back into a creative groove, he soon became a Safe Place regular. Much of Bang's writing employs irony and wit to make social commentary, all of it firmly rooted in his immigrant experience and Asian identity. His writing is also influenced by performance poetry, and often written to be heard. And Bang knows how to command an audience. In Safe Place, his deadpan deliveries of his funniest pieces are particularly appreciated.

Regret, pain and sorrow . . . a ghost you chase down the night halls of your memories.

Bang Nguyen

NO, THAT'S MY NAME . . .

It's Bong with an *A*, not b*Ang*. No, it sounds like b*Ong*, but with an *A*. Yah, yah, like a water bong, or the sound of a gong, bOng! It's got an *A*, not an *O*. You have to stretch the *A*. B*aaa*ng. In Vietnamese it means equal. Not anything fancy like Equality and Liberty. It's more common, like "same." Like these two are the same, or we are the same. My whole name in Vietnamese means, "Man of the people among them," and goes all the way back to ancient Vietnam.

Anyways, we're just talking about the Americanized way to say my name. In my language it's not even said this way. There's a whole lot of accent marks missing in your American language. The *A* should have an accent mark like a bamboo hat over it. It's from the French Indo-China times and makes the *A* sound low, then high, then low again, all in one letter. No, your language is too flat to say it. No way, you can't pronounce it.

OK, OK. Bâng . . . No, lower, then higher, lower. Start with a dip, go up, then pull back. Bâng . . . Forget it. Let's talk about something else, and you can practice later. And no, I don't want to get stoned 'cuz of my name!

Bang Nguyen

AA HAATERS

"Gook! Boater! F.O.B!"
"Go home Viet Cong!"
That's when I'd start to erupt with tears.
I was home!
Punch! Kick! Punch!
"Take it back!"
Punch! Punch! Punch!
"Waah . . . STOP! STOP! You Chink!"
"Ahaa! You're a Chink too!!"

Growing up in Seattle as refugees from the Vietnam War,
the established young Asians resented us newcomers.
Now there was someone else to be blamed and bullied
on the playground because they didn't fit in.
Yet. Because haters gotta hate. Asian on Asian haters.
Yep, back then, AA meant something totally different to me.

Bang Nguyen

LOST AND FOUND

Now largely obscured by layers of concert ads,
a huge tattered poster wraps end to end on a street pole.
It's been there for a long time. Years. In big loud letters
it reads, LOST: JOB. CAR. HOME. Job last seen,
downsized, near an industry black hole in the 2008
financial crisis. Car and Home dependent on Job.

Neighbors report, Car last seen with a sturdy man
holding large metal leash, leaning down to shackle
its underside. Home last seen with sturdy man's partner,
dressed in a slick suit, holding an
electronic padlock, and waving legal documents.
Overheard telling Home,
"You're mine now! I got you at auction!"

Down at the bottom of the poster tattered tear-away tabs read:
"Please tear another piece of me off for yourself."

But what's this?
On a pole further down the road, another poster,
fresh and simple among the clutter, it reads:
FOUND. Resolution. Presence. Peace of Mind.
No need to keep looking for my stuff.
I'VE FOUND MYSELF.

Bang Nguyen

SMOKE AND MIRRORS

You grow up hard together,
so you're only soft with each other.
When you're friends with needy gangsters
and proud addicts, you can have really bad life advice.

Deep in the mystic cloud of fellowship and loyalty
it's hard to see outside of it. Only if and when
you step away far from this false shroud
covering your path can you realize
it's all smoke and mirrors. Then it's like Bruce Lee
at the end of *Enter the Dragon,* when he breaks
his way through the house of mirrors
to freedom.

Bang Nguyen

MY FAMILY COLLECTION

My dad's used silver Mercedes-Benz basic 190E, on an immigrant business man's budget, to class up for his buddies to follow after. My mom's accompanying imitation, wood-paneled, Chevy Malibu Station Wagon tank, seated a refugee clan of two families: up to twenty, if you know how to maximize every square inch, like the Third World does.

My brother's sexual, chocolate brown Nissan Maxima was my dad's hand-me-down, but fully loaded with a gazillion speakers and gadgets that fried the car's electronics every time he took it out to impress everyone on the Alki Beach cruising strip, though he always had to get a jump start from a more practical Asian friend with a simple Datsun Chinese delivery econo-box.

I inherited my brother's hand-me-down, a Honda CRX "sports," a practical hatchback. It was Honda's conservative and compromised first attempt at entering the sports car market. But it got twenty-five miles per gallon and had the best emissions in its class—for sports cars. I drove this secondhand, second class, two seater "sports car" around for a while. Like clothes, you either took the hand-me-downs or went without.

But for me this was my first car. This little blue Autobot was mine, a "rice burner" to class up, race and cruise the strip. So, okay, I drove it. Raced and cruised the strip in my blue and grey college hatchback mini-fridge with Matchbox car toy wheels, classed up with the practical package of Pimp-My-Ride back window shades, along with a Japanese business man's notion of a back spoiler.

And my Asian friends, with their Jap econo-cars, would be like, "Fresh man! You got a C-R-X, that's the SHIIT!"

While the white jocks with their muscle cars were, "Why don't you get a real car, not that rice burner?"

But the homies with their land yacht hoopties were perplexed: "I don't get it, it's so small. How you gonna party with your posse on Broadway?"

Bang Nguyen

STRANGE HOMECOMING

"That was the Bauhaus Cafe! See, the front door frame
still looks like it sorta . . . I know, it's gone . . .
And that used to be . . . I know, it's gone too.

"Oh, that's the block that used to be Tugs gay bar
next to King Cobra the Irish bar. I know, it's gone.
And that was Bill's Pizza . . . well, that huge hole used to be Bill's.
You can still tell because next door is Linda's Tavern,
the only place still here."

"Whoa! You don't recognize anything?"

"No, man! It's just terraformed and replaced,
an alien urban landscape."

You can live half your life growing up in a neighborhood,
intimate with every street corner and alley.
Then you leave, like Jason and the Argonauts,
off on a fantastic journey to explore the world beyond.
An epic adventure to breathe adventure into your life,
like wind into sails, all of it taking you further
and further away from home and that young man
who was once "from around the way."

Many lives later, you return to the port of your youth,
a world-weary traveler, counting on the familiar old hood
to be there, waiting patiently for you,
like a loyal pet, unflinching and unfazed by time.

Then whoa! The shock of so much change!
Your familiar stomping grounds now unrecognizable
with you a stranger in a strange land.

Ok, so it's time to reflect on your own self,
like taking a deep look into a pool,
except, the deeper you look the stranger it gets.

"Hey stranger, you from around here?"

"No, not anymore. I'm just visiting."

Bang Nguyen

NOT MY BROTHER
(from *Another American Dream)*

We started out the same. Born in the same coastal city in Vietnam,
the sons of sisters from our mothers' side. Refugees on the same boat
from Saigon to Seattle. We went to the same schools,
in the same graduating class, got jobs,
and began climbing the corporate ladder.

We were more like brothers than cousins.

But somehow, I couldn't keep climbing.
It seemed the higher I climbed the more the burden
of guilt weighed on me for my executive decisions.
Did I say execute?
I felt like a financial hit man. A corporate bankster.
Everything started to look slick on me.
Slick hair. Slick suits. Slick style.
I was fast becoming a corporate burnout,
my business life an infamous two pots of coffee morning,
two martini lunch, and way more than two hours of happy hour
each and every day.

I got caught in a rung, and fell off the corporate ladder.

Unlike me, Cousin showed no sign of cracking. He was busy,
doing the same thing in pharmaceuticals I'd done in banking
while still looking like a post-college fresh intern: like the token
Asian walk-on to a *Friends* episode. Always. The fresh
clean-cut, barber-clipped hair, the white and blue striped
Seinfeld button-up shirt, the Dockers and loafers combo.
The perfect stereotype of the overly Asian nice guy.

Who could guess the real man
underneath all those layers of pop TV sitcom demeanor?
A cold, calculating killer for the company with a career
of making pharmaceutical decisions of how to cut corners on
patients' meds; how to keep chemo patients' spreadsheets
profitable; how to retain company costs by shorting dying
cancer patients on their death beds.

You've heard of the American sicko?
Well, here was the American psycho.
My fresh and so clean-cut Cousin now the Hannibal Lecter
of the Western States Region of a major multinational pharmaceutical.

All of it became very real to me and my siblings
a few years ago when our father landed in the hospital
with a surprising diagnosis of cancer
and was dead within the month. Those last couple of days
his only relief was from cancer pain killers
the doctors administered. And that's when it clicked
just what our cousin did for a living.
That's when we finally saw through his costume.

Bang Nguyen

THE KISS

One last, long, make-out kiss and I let her out of the car, walked her to the house, and helped prop her up to sneak back in her bedroom window. "Good night, honey," I whispered to my third date of the night. I never call them by their first names; it's too hard to keep track of all the names when you're juggling a dozen girlfriends.

I revved the motor on my Trans Am and spun out of the neighborhood for home. Racing across town, trying to beat the sunrise and my parents from catching me. The fat racing tires of my Trans Am rolled slow and heavy across our crunchy gravel driveway. When only the birds are awake, the world can hear your every noise and my gears were grinding. I was real late—or early. I'd lost my pinks to the morning sun.

I tiptoed to the back door. This opened onto the laundry room, with my attic loft room directly above. This had been strategically fought over with all my other siblings so that, like a ninja, I could sneak in and out to hang with my "G's" and my ladies. Yes, I was a real bad thug lover. I cracked the screen door, then wiggled the locks to the back door, and I was in!

Uh oh! To my surprise, the laundry room door to the kitchen was wide open, with my father leaning over a cutting board on the kitchen counter, chopping and cooking the rare Dad's family breakfast. He looked up slowly: "Boy, where have you been?!"

"I don't have to tell you, old man.
I'm stronger, younger, smarter . . ."

THUNK!! The kitchen knife flew across the room and half way into the wall, mere inches to the right of my heart. "Boy, you don't know anything. I have lived ten times more than you ever have. Or will."

Years later, I learned from my father's Vietnam Vet buddies that he'd served as second in command of a Special Forces Navy Seal Base in the Mekong Delta, was at the Fall of Saigon, and had been the biggest playboy, not just in his graduating class, or his military base, but in the WHOLE of the Vietnam-based Navy.

Be careful of those long kisses good night.

Bang Nguyen

TO STRESS

Stress, you drive my past,
present, and future.
You've been there for me
in the worse of times,
and sometimes the best.
You weren't always welcome
but you came along anyways.
Stress, you were there for me
when Grandma passed,
when Dad passed.
Will you be there when I pass?
I think so. You're always present
except, when I'm present,
have presence of mind,
when I meditate.
Where are you then, stress?
Where are you / do you go
when I am happy?

Bang Nguyen

PAST AND PRESENT

Was,
best in class to chug 40's
best in class to snort everything
best in class to live fast, die young!

Was,
best corporate banker of the year
best speakeasy nightclub owner of the year
best overdose scene on Capitol Hill—EVER!

Now,
simply a good volunteer, activist, barista, and Paleo cook
simply, a dedicated pupil in yoga and meditation,
simply giving back.

Megan McInnis

Megan was born and raised in Issaquah, Washington. A classically-trained singer, she had an early career as a songwriter and performer of deliciously satirical songs with the band Lava Toad. (It is no exaggeration to say that listening to Megan sing "Large Dead Bird" will lift any Thanksgiving celebration to new and hilarious levels while simultaneously knocking the stuffing out of any puritan hanger-on types.) Yet, already, mental illness and addiction were upending her life. Some bleak years followed.

For Megan, reclaiming herself as an artist is essential to her recovery. Writing creatively plays an important role in this, and she has been in my classroom and a part of Safe Place from the start. She also loves, and reads, literature (lots of it), and this is reflected in her writing. She finds stories everywhere and in every prompt. In Safe Place, her personal essays pour themselves onto the page almost fully-formed and always beautifully structured. Her language usage is witty and crisp. Megan also creates a character out of herself. In writing about her life and experience, she both inhabits and relives the experience, while also "stepping outside" of herself to observe her own behavior and quirks. This, in turn, often lends itself to humor, even in situations that weren't funny at the time, and Megan's appreciation of the absurd is often evidenced in her writing.

Within the group, Megan's keen ear and attentiveness, along with her literary background, benefits everyone. In giving others feedback, she is both caring and insightful, and her observations help everyone learn. And every once in a while, if a prompt is music-based, she may treat us to a song.

I couldn't have met myself at the door because I didn't know where I lived.

Megan McInnis

BREAD

With my dad gone, my mom fed us perfectly well on $4 a week from the State, plus basics like flour and salt from the food bank. Back then, she says, they were nothing like today's food banks with fresh milk and produce and more kinds of bread than even Thriftway used to have. The advantage, at least for me, was that my mom baked all our bread—and enough that we never ran out of food.

Every breakfast was Red Rose Tea and toast—sometimes egg on toast. That meant a poached egg mashed with a fork and spread out to every corner, then peppered and cut into nine even squares. Egg or no egg, the toast was buttered from crust to crust and served on my Raggedy Ann Plate with the crack down the middle. One day my mother asked if I'd ever like something different from tea and toast and I said no, just tea and toast.

On Saturdays she put my tea in a bottle and got me up impossibly early for the garage sales. I didn't mind being seen by grown-ups, but if there were kids I hid behind her leg; I didn't like other kids to see me at three-years-old sucking a bottle. Strangely, I never tried just hiding the bottle. It didn't occur to me to stop drinking for even a minute, so I was forced to hide myself.

All other mornings we ate at the wooden table in the breakfast nook on the built-in wooden benches. The table and benches were lacquered so thickly with shiny white paint that I could make little crescent-shaped dents with my thumbnail. When I found a paint brush hair stuck in the back rest, which formed the wall behind me, and carefully peeled the hair away, it left a faint, thin trace like a fossil. The tablecloth was checkered: alternating squares of solid red, solid white, and what I thought of as red-and-white sprinkled. It was plastic, but textured to resemble a weave. I was pleased by the similarity between the tablecloth and my blue-and-white nightgown in the same checkered pattern; the sameness seemed like a surprising and lucky coincidence.

Next to my Raggedy Ann Plate of toast went my tea in the bluebird cup: a rounded, nearly antique mug from Goodwill, whitish with a soft glaze and, perched on the rim above the handle, a bluebird that was also a whistle. I got to pour my own milk, and I watched it cloud up in the tea before I stirred in the sugar. Then my mom squeezed in two drops of a liquid multivitamin; she took a shiny yellow pill that I knew was Geritol but that looked so much like an M&M I'd been forced to try it, just once. It didn't taste one bit like an M&M.

I don't remember missing or craving more exotic foods, except for Jell-O Cheesecake, which I could have eaten every day, but I know I enjoyed the regional dishes available at the homes of my relatives. My Aunt Maureen (Mama's sister), two streets down, had sourdough bread—not homemade, but delicious as toast or in a tomato sandwich with mayonnaise and pepper. Her family ate it with guava jelly and Tillamook Cheddar, which didn't appeal to me, but we all loved peanut butter and banana (not on sourdough but on regular Wonder Bread).

My grandmother, on the other side of the family and the other side of town, baked bread like my mom, but hers was whole wheat. That was fine—healthy, but not creepy like some of the other things my dad's family exposed me to. Wheatgrass, for instance—they made a thing in the blender they called "green drink," but that didn't change what it was: grass juice. One of my hippie aunts said I couldn't have a peanut butter and jelly sandwich until I'd drunk a whole glass of it, but I could barely manage a sip. (Safely back with my maternal family after this kind of episode, I related every ghastly detail. Maureen, especially, was morbidly fascinated with my reports of that family's culinary atrocities.)

That was more typical of my dad and his sisters; Grandma was relatively safe, with more old-fashioned ideas of health and nutrition. And really, her whole wheat bread was delicious—well-toasted and saturated with butter (it took a lot because the bread was so dense), then piled with as much honey as surface tension allowed. Her bread contained hard, chewy bits that must have been wheat berries or some kind of seed, and were satisfying to squash between my teeth.

Grandma's house had tea, but didn't revolve around it—and the tea was Lipton instead of Red Rose. In place of sugar, she had honey, which she apparently thought of as healthier even in unlimited quantities; she kept a half-gallon can right out on the counter. (Right under the counter, she kept a half-gallon jug of red wine, and all day long she sat in one corner of the green davenport sipping it out of a child's plastic juice cup.)

Grandma also kept special treats like a bag of Fun-Size Snickers in the freezer. My cousin Erika, naturally skinny and therefore superior, was in charge of asking permission for us to eat them—never more than one each day. (On my own, I would have kept asking all day, and then would have stopped even asking.) Sometimes Erika tormented me by secretly saving her Snickers while I ate mine, then producing it later and eating in front of me—sometimes hours later. This steely self-control was another proof of her superiority.

But my Aunt Maureen's was where I went most often: she babysat me and I played with my Cousin Eric while my mom went to Bellevue Community College or was called in as a substitute school bus driver. (Eric was one year minus-ten-days older than Erika, with me in between.) Because of my Uncle Will's job at the bus garage, Maureen could afford all kinds of things: Product 19, Eggo's Frozen Waffles, tuna fish, Vernor's Ginger Ale (based in Detroit, my mom's home town), and sometimes Fudgsicles. Eric and I had a ritual for treats like Fudgsicles, Dreamsicles, and cake batter beaters: whoever finished first began a taunting call-and-response: "I-I bea-eat," followed by "I get the mo-ost," repeated as often as necessary. I never said so, but I always thought of "beating" as a hollow victory next to getting the most.

At Maureen's house, there was so much food that the only limit was my mother's reminder to leave them enough milk for tea in the morning. At Maureen's house, there was so much food that, unlike at home, I was always hungry.

Megan McInnis

THE KINDNESS OF STRANGERS

I have always depended on the kindness of strangers.
—Blanche DuBois

The first time I came to the Recovery Café, I was sick to my stomach. Having lived for ten years in isolation, going almost anywhere made me sick to my stomach. For a time, I'd get sick to my stomach just getting in line at the supermarket; I was scared to talk to the cashier.

Fortunately, no one at the bus stop tried to talk to me. Like typical strangers, the waiting passengers gave me and each other more than enough space. Perhaps we do this out of mistrust, or shyness, or even what might be considered respect: "I won't talk to you if you don't talk to me. It's only polite—and, besides, you might ask for money."

Especially on the bus, this distancing is critical: we're trapped. Avoiding eye contact is a matter of life and death. You may not escape having someone sit next to you, but at least you can discourage conversation.

I don't exactly approve of this unfriendliness, but I can't quite condemn it. I once had to sit near a guy who, after asking what I was reading, reached out to borrow it, flipped through the pages, and read parts aloud, making comments. (I wasn't surprised when he mentioned he'd recently quit taking lithium.) That's the kind of thing that can happen if you look up even once.

Getting off the bus in Seattle, I was safe again: even when I glanced at other people they wouldn't look back. It was reassuring but also kind of hurt my feelings, because I almost wanted to smile at a few of them but they wouldn't even meet my eye. I have to admit I didn't try very hard; the odds of rejection were high, and I couldn't afford to be cavalier.

For the first few blocks, the streets were owned by business people. They moved in gangs, speaking powerfully, on their way to meet powerful people at power lunches. You could almost see the cubicles they'd built around themselves, moving along with them to keep out all irrelevancies. (Others walked singly, with headsets, focusing just as intently to the exclusion of their surroundings. Their juxtaposition with the mentally ill, who also conversed with invisible people, was nothing short of eerie.) Concerning the mutual lack of acknowledgment between these people and me, my feelings were unmixed, containing no tinge of the regret I normally have in not connecting.

Besides all the business folk were other people with haircuts and outfits or attractive dogs or well-dressed babies, and they, too, seemed self-contained. That wasn't so bad. It was being ignored by the streetwise, hard-living crowd that bothered me most, because I imagined they had the contempt for me that I had for the powerful people. I wanted to say, "I have street cred. I've lived in a car and peed outside and been harassed by cops. I only look like this 'cause my mom buys me clothes." I wanted these people's approval—so it still came to that. I wanted someone outside my head to tell me I had a right to exist.

After seven blocks I turned a corner and there it was. Not the Recovery Café—I hadn't noticed it yet, across the street—but something almost as solid and palpable. I thought of the promised land of the Mouse Reepicheep, from the *Narnia* series: "Where sky and water meet, / where the waves grow sweet . . ." The waves had grown sweet. The people around this corner were happy, and friendly—if not directly to me, then to each other—and I didn't feel like they were trying to keep that energy *from* me. Some of them, when I passed, still had their smiles from the last contact, and didn't put them away.

The closer I got to the building, the more people nodded at me or said Hi. Someone held the door open—not out of obligation but more like he knew me. The desk people smiled like they'd been expecting me—not like the "greeters" in certain stores, who are really just watchers. When someone asked if he could help me, it wasn't a euphemism for, "Look, we can both pretend you came here by mistake, and you can leave unescorted if you leave *now.*"

It turned out this cheerfulness didn't come only from the people with nametags. Others were walking around or sitting at tables talking together or laughing, or yelling across the room to each other like longtime friends at a party. And when I squeezed in beside a guy to get coffee, or asked where to put my empty cup, they were as welcoming as if they knew I'd arrived with one of their friends. Some offered their names and asked for mine, as if taking for granted they'd see me again. I was already in.

When I left that day I was like the people I'd seen when I came: smiling at all the other members coming and going, and feeling a smile at the ready, just behind my face, for a long time after.

Walking back to the bus stop—sometimes bursting into a run—here and there I tried to catch someone's eye and smile at them, but they looked away for the most part, almost as if to save me embarrassment for what might have been a facial tic. Sometimes just before looking away they smiled kind of curtly (or that's how I took it), not quite meeting my eye. That shook my confidence a little, because I'd only just *barely* started recovering, and things like that still hurt. But that day was a turning point, and it marked an important new stage of my recovery.

I have never depended on the kindness of strangers, but I'm finally starting to.

Megan McInnis

APPLYING MYSELF

I already knew it was coming. For seven years—since the day I got the award letter saying that, yes, I was crazy enough to get $1,200 a month from the State until my next evaluation came—I knew the evaluation would come.

It had been a nightmare to fill out the eight-page application insisting I wasn't fit for work. The hardest question was on the first page: "Describe what you do from the time you wake up until you go to bed." I swear, in the seven weeks I spent slaving over that form (including the three-week extension I asked for), I could have responded, "I try to answer this question."

I still have a notebook in which I drafted replies: thirty-six pages containing more than two hundred possible opening lines or paragraphs. And that's not including the hundreds of drafts on other pieces of paper I later threw away.

More than thirty attempts began, "Increasingly, my schedule is dictated by my OCD." Other versions went something like, "My schedule varies according to the focus of my OCD, with one constant: two to four hours daily, in separate incidents, of excessive grooming and related acts of self-harm, sometimes causing mild but lasting damage."

My boyfriend kept saying that I should include all the drafts of my answer in the envelope along with the form, but my OCD made that idea repellent; it seemed too disorganized. I think what won my case, though, were the layers and layers of Wite-Out on top of which I wrote in a tiny script, filling two lines of space for each printed line, and often continuing onto the back of the page with another two paragraphs.

It was either that or the form sent in by my psychiatrist, listing diagnoses he'd never told me about and I would only learn about six years after applying, when he retired and sent me my nine years of records. Not just OCD and depression, which I'd already known about, but two others: bipolar and borderline. Bipolar? Hmm, interesting. BORDERLINE? I looked it up in *DSM IV.* Sure enough, I fit seven of the nine criteria.

Still, I was hurt that he'd labeled me that way. Maybe it was because I told him exactly why I'd been fired from my last job (that thing about the $10,000), and that I now lived in a car. Or that I'd supported myself and my boyfriend—rent, food, utilities, methadone treatment—by stealing department store jewelry and selling it on eBay. (eBay . . . the world's greatest fence.) But, wait—I hadn't even told him that part. And he said I was borderline anyway.

But that was back then. Over the years I've gotten much better, thanks to medication, therapy, and leaving a codependent relationship with a boyfriend who never held a job or even lifted a finger to help me with shoplifting. For several years my psychiatrists have told me it might be good to get back in the workforce. And two weeks ago I got my reevaluation form from Social Security.

I know that my new psychiatrist won't agree to submit the forms saying I'm still disabled. I know that I'm not still disabled; I've even started applying for jobs. But it's one thing to try to convince someone you're pathetic and crazy; now I have to prove I'm competent—and list all the places I've worked in the last five years.

It's been more than ten. And the last place, I was fired for gross misconduct.

Proving my competence is gonna be a lot harder.

Megan McInnis

FINDING HIGHER POWERS

1.

Practicing

Being an atheist isn't all fun and games. Being an atheist and sober is barely tolerable; that's why six-and-a-half of the Twelve Steps require a spiritual commitment. They say you don't have to believe in God to do the steps—it's just *God as you understand him*—but I don't understand him at all.

I've tried to believe in a power greater than myself, besides DSHS, but I can't feel anything—although I feel deeply for certain overtly fictional characters, in a way that perhaps could *only* be described as spiritual. It's possible that art and music and literature have brought me closer than anything else, besides acid, to understanding spirituality.

But praying—don't get me started. That's like dressing up for a date you don't even have: sure, you can tell yourself someone is there when you open the door, but you're not gonna make yourself believe it.

Or so I *thought*, until recently.

I won't try to justify this or transfer the blame; let's just say I got mixed up in a certain crowd and one thing led to another and suddenly there I was: in church. I can't explain it, any more than I can explain the fact that, barely a week later, there I was again, back for more. So it's been about a year now, and I'm not any closer to God than I was before but, as habits go, it could be worse. At least I'm a functioning churchgoer.

But that's getting ahead of myself. Unsurprisingly, perhaps, my experimenting didn't end there; instead it was more of a gateway. Turns out my pastor's involved in a pretty big operation on the side, known as the Recovery Café. This place is notorious for giving free meals and free classes to the homeless, the jobless; the disowned, the disabled, the dissed; hardened criminals, softened criminals, and drug addicts. There wasn't a category there I didn't fit.

So I signed up—just for a harmless writing class (none of the hard stuff). Later I got roped into running dishes—not every day, just here and there. But I kept hearing about this other class, "Meditation and the Five Elements"— meaning the elements earth, fire, water, air, and ether. The one that interested me, of course, was the ether, and I wondered if it was the reason that everyone who went into that class came out looking unmistakably calm. I decided to give it a try. Nothing wrong with a little social meditating once a week—and I could always quit anytime.

But, sure enough, I started meditating at home, by myself. I was even inhaling. Deeply inhaling and exhaling, up to half an hour a day. Then twice a day. Then constantly. Suddenly I was smack in the middle of a hardcore, two-hundred-mantra-a-day habit.

There were the Guru, Ganesh, and Gayatri Mantras. The Shakti and Shanti Mantras. The first-in-the-morning and last-in-the evening mantras, whatever I could sneak in on a trip to the bathroom, and the 108 mantras to go with the 108 beads on a mala.

What I liked about the mala was its resemblance to a rosary. Catholicism is so artistically beautiful and so mentally destructive that it became almost like a fetish for me to emulate it while simultaneously profaning it.

My mother was raised by Catholics, beaten by her father at home and at school by the nuns, and essentially forced by a priest to deliver her only-begotten bastard son into the lap of a holier family (a cruelty unsurprising in a clergy that with one hand curses homosexuality and, with the other, coerces altar boys).

Of course this sounds anti-Christian. Of course it is. But I'm not completely intolerant: I say, cheers to Christ, jeers to Christianity. Especially the kind that's turned Jesus from the hippie I knew as a child, ready to turn the other cheek or burn his draft card, to the Fundamentalist bodybuilder of today, more anxious to kick some Muslim ass.

You might assume my aversion to spirituality stems from resentment, but that's not true: what I resent is not being able to believe. There's no comfort in atheism. I even took another class, "Living Deeply," to see if I could *learn* to believe in something. When the teacher assigned us to write about our spiritual practices, I thought I wouldn't be able to because I didn't have any. It took me a second to realize the whole meditation thing with the gurus and gods and goddesses would technically be considered spiritual.

The reason it took me a second was the very fact that I didn't believe in it, but then I had to consider that I *was* still doing it, even after learning we wouldn't get to inhale ether.

Plus there was the fact that I was still going to church.

So I realized I *do* have a spiritual practice. But I'm the reverse of a lot of people who say things like, "I'm a Christian, I just don't go to church," or "I don't go to church but I follow the Ten Commandments" (which strikes out the fourth one right there), or that bumper-sticker, "I'm not religious, I just love the Lord." Well, I'm the opposite: I'm not a Christian, I don't believe in God, but I go to church every Sunday and pray in Sanskrit *religiously* every day. You could say I'm a church-going, Brahma-worshipping atheist, and I'd be hard put to prove otherwise.

It's working pretty well for me so far.

2.

Hundreds of Ways to Kiss the Ground

Let the beauty we love be what we do.
There are hundreds of ways to kneel and kiss the ground.—Rumi

Amazing that an Eastern mystic has the very words to express my realization that Eastern philosophy isn't for me. Truth hides in so many places, and there are so many ways to get to the truth, but my own path, I've learned, is not through the East. It seems that my truth lies deep in the roots of my own Whitey heritage.

By that I don't mean Whitey religion—Holy Mother of God, not by all the saints in heaven. I mean the small-town, lower-middle class lifestyle I grew up with. I no longer want to get in the shower and pray to Goddess Kali to remove my negativity through the de-charging element of water: *Om Nama Shivaya, Om Nama Shivaya.* I no longer want to perform the Sun Salute in honor of gods I don't believe in any more than I believe in the Christian God.

I want to dance to the Andrews Sisters and Hot Lips Page and Cab Calloway . . . well, maybe it's not just my Whitey heritage, but the Western heritage that's a part of me I just can't shake. And why should I shake it? I want to shake it to Carmen Miranda. I want to sing to hot jazz from the 30s and 40s. That's who I am. That's my nature. I've been ignoring my nature too long.

I don't mind going back to yoga, maybe, now that I've spent the last few months getting it out of my system—the part that wasn't me. I'll take it on again, but not like before. I don't want to chant. I don't want to sit in a room with sincere believers and sing to Ganesh as if I, too, believed in a fat blue elephant with too many arms. I just don't. Why pretend I do?

I believe in joy. I believe in singing and dancing and art. I believe in an hour of grueling uphill pedaling for a five-minute downhill flight, screaming with euphoria.

I believe in kindness. I believe in smiling at strangers even after the last one didn't smile back. I believe in accepting people who do believe in blue elephants or virgin mothers or saints, or don't know what to believe. I believe in finding my own truth, and not dismissing it on the assumption that someone else's truth is truer, just because it isn't mine.

I was raised to wait for someone to come along and show me someplace to get to—help me to see through the distance. Now I realize there are hundreds of ways to kneel and kiss the ground.

Tamar Hirsch

Tamar was born in Jerusalem, into an Orthodox Jewish family. She grew up in Los Angeles, California, with a childhood punctuated by trauma and long stays in state institutions. Her father was a Holocaust survivor and her mother was the child of Holocaust survivors. The "Holocaust Cloud" (as Tamar calls it) always seemed to be present in some form or other. Her early love of books and reading helped her get through some dark times, and fueled a life-long love affair with words, word play, and writing.

I met Tamar in the spring of 2012, in the first class I taught at the Café. When it ended, she was among those urging me to continue. She has been a part of Safe Place from the very beginning. During the four years I've known her, two key decisions dramatically changed her life and have aided her recovery. The first was switching to a gluten- and dairy-free diet. The second was going back to school to finish her degree—which was possible because her overall health and energy levels were so much better due to her change in diet! She has been happy to discover that she excels at academics, and made it onto the Dean's List and Honor Society at her community college; she is now a student at Seattle University.

In Safe Place, Tamar's delightfully quirky and original sense of humor often shows up in her writing, even when writing about things that were far from funny at the time, and she is a big fan of the healing power of laughter. Mostly she writes poetry, but sometimes finds prose more suited to her serious side and moods.

A new beginning doesn't have to start in January.

Tamar Hirsch

FOOTPRINT

It has taken me
all of forty years
to comprehend
my future, and
to accept
that I have gifts.
I have been humbled.
Working hard
for what my soul
desires
is a present
I give myself.

A desert
drenched with rain
can dry out. Nothing
is permanent.
Because I started
where I once ended,
I can now leave
a footprint.

Tamar Hirsch

ADVICE TO MYSELF

Slow down.
Everything doesn't have to be
accomplished right now.
Snuggling the cats for a few extra minutes
is worth getting a late start.
Bring my lunch, gluten and dairy free.
Remember, humor heals me.
Don't be an ass. Include donkeys
in my research paper about animal therapy.
Remember, family
does not have to be related
and my friends value me.
Spending time alone
does not make me lonely.
Walk up the hill . . .
though carrying 20 lbs of cat litter
needs to be planned.
Fill the refrigerator with food
that replenishes my soul.
Remember, my journey
will always be changing and
I'm okay the way I am now.

Tamar Hirsch

HOLOCAUST CLOUD

Sadness was just a part of everyday life growing up. Some things were talked about and some things were forbidden to talk about. Nevertheless, they were very loud in their silence. The Holocaust was one of those forbidden topics in my home. However, in our living room was a framed Jewish star that said *Juif* in French. It was worn by a great uncle, and a few years after World War II found in a Hebrew prayer book given to my grandmother; it was one of the few possessions that survived while the family didn't.

The framed star was hung amongst other artwork and tapestries. When I was a kid I didn't grasp the magnitude of how horrific the Holocaust was. But the Jewish star definitely didn't belong next to a bunch of celebratory art. Only when I was old enough and bold enough to ask why it looked like a framed piece of art did I receive a defensive reply that, "It was framed so we wouldn't forget this horrible time in history." I certainly could never have forgotten, even though I was not alive during World War II.

My father was born during the Holocaust in Germany. His father, my grandfather, was in a concentration camp for much of my father's childhood. On the rare occasion that I saw my grandparents or uncles and aunt on my father's side, the sadness that permeated the air was enough to choke on—just like a closed room of chain smokers. There were no hugs, no gifts exchanged, just a Holocaust cloud looming over us.

Tamar Hirsch

MY FATHER'S VISIT

The first week of the winter quarter, pneumonia hijacked my body. I was miserable and not even my cats brought comfort because my hacking cough startled them. Not only did I feel physically incapacitated, I also felt emotionally paralyzed. I couldn't stop thinking about how much I was missing in school, and how I would never be able to catch up. Of course, other self-depreciating thoughts invaded my mind also.

I only looked at my email a few times, and when I saw the email from my father that he was coming to Seattle for four hours the following Sunday, I immediately felt even more overwhelmed. I was afraid my debilitating physical state would not improve and I would have a four hour marathon coughing session and not be able to talk or even go anywhere.

My father, who lives in Israel, has never seen me in a healthy manner. I wanted this visit to be different. My whole life he has always had to "fix" things, and be the one who got me out of bad situations, like landlord problems, cars impounded, taking care of things while I spent time in numerous psychiatric hospitals for cutting and suicide attempts.

The Sunday my father arrived in Seattle I was feeling much better, and was excited to show him the life that I have created. The visit was very brief, but it was the most meaningful time I've ever had with him. First stop was showing him my art that was on display in the Washington State Convention Center. Since traveling around and getting to and from the airport took up so much time, we only had a brief amount of time left. I took him to my school, Seattle University, next. We went into my home away from home, the library. In violation of the "Quiet Zone" no talking sign, we sat and talked in the reading room next to the original Matisse hanging on the wall.

Instead of talking about things—such as that I really needed to live in a residential facility, get my act together, and not do detrimental things to myself—we talked about all the things I've accomplished on my own. Here I was, sitting in a $50,000-a-year university that my father and no-one else has helped me with. I felt on top of the world (or on top of a stack of books . . .). I also shared my piece that was in *Raven Chronicles Magazine* this past summer. Although he didn't get my word play, he still seemed to enjoy that my writing was published.

Since we had very little time left, we took a quick picture by my favorite fountain before we walked across the street and waited for his taxi. Just before the taxi arrived my father told me he was proud of me. I had never heard those words from him before. I don't know when or if I'll ever see him again, but at least I was finally able to show my father that I'd fixed myself.

Tamar Hirsch

CAPTURE THE FLAG

Capture the Flag was something I played for the first time in the state hospital when I was a kid. Being outside was a privilege I had to earn. The manure-filled air seemed so much more enjoyable when I was rarely allowed outside!

The game consisted of two teams of two or three, depending on who else earned their privileges. I honestly can't remember the game, except we had to pull a bright orange flag which was Velcroed to something, and then run. Running was something I was good at because I escaped quite a few times. However, I soon discovered that I was faster running without permission!

The game wasn't important. What mattered was I got out of the confines of the stuffy, overmedicated unit and was able to grasp moments of a normal childhood. I was free, until the flag was captured and I got brought back to my cage.

Tamar Hirsch

FIT FOR A KING

The dentist told me to be still
so he could make
an impression for a crown.
Be still? A crown?
I couldn't control myself.
I pulled out the cotton that
was cushioning my tooth.
I asked if I had to
make a good impression
for royalty?

The dentist and his assistant
laughed and the cotton
was put back in my mouth.

Most people loath going to
the dentist because of the pain.
I dread going to the dentist
because I can't talk.
The numbing shot is not as
agonizing as having to be
silent while a juicy conversation
is taking place
over my tongue-tied mouth.

I left with my temporary
crown and was on the prowl
for some stimulating dialogue
but I sounded unintelligible
given my anesthesic
predicament.

I was uncrowned a day later
in an unfair manner.
A piece of obstinate spinach
unblended in my Smoothie
dethroned me.

My mouth and I are back
to being a common person,
awaiting my permanent
sovereignty.

Tamar Hirsch

FOOD DILEMMAS

Being gluten- and dairy-free has brought up all kinds of food memories from growing up in a kosher home. I have to look at labels carefully, because sometimes something is gluten-free, but often there's some hidden dairy ingredient. This is similar to when I was a kid and something looked tasty, and my dad would have to look into the ingredients to make sure there wasn't some hidden, un-kosher ingredient.

Being hungry and wanting to eat something quickly has taken on a whole new element. I no longer can run into a store and buy something that's delicious but incredibly bad for me. Last night was one of those nights. I was running from class to class and then had a lengthy bus ride to get to the Apple store in the University Village for a computer lesson. I hadn't eaten more than a handful of nuts all day. I was no longer hungry and felt like I was floating. My head was killing me.

So I went into a market with a gluten-free friend of mine. We walked past all these pastries, and the sugar and fruity smells high-jacked my nose. We discussed my gastrointestinal consequences and the excessive itching my friend experienced if she ate baked goods. We walked around the store, and everything that was no longer part of my diet seemed to jump out at me. I looked at all the cheeses and kept reminding myself how I would feel if I ate any of them. We dutifully went to the unappetizing gluten-free section. I was able to stay on track, and bought some cardboard-tasting gluten-free crackers and some hummus. But at the last minute my friend gave into temptation and bought a whole cake, and said she would just deal with her itching.

Tamar Hirsch

GASTROINTESTINAL SUFFOCATION

A buffet is generally not the ideal place for a vegetarian to eat. Going to a buffet as a gluten- and dairy-free vegetarian is like going to Alaska with a surfboard. This July 4th my friend dragged me along to a "cheap" buffet. $16.95 was not cheap for some wilted lettuce, baby corn, cherry tomatoes, and three small pieces of pineapple. Looking around, everyone else was piling their plates as high as the Leaning Tower of Pisa. So just to fit in, I piled my cherry tomatoes on top of the baby corn, and stacked my pineapple.

Meanwhile, my friend was enjoying her second plate of crab legs, Chinese food, and enough starchy food to glue anyone's stomach together.

For me, there was no temptation except for the berry cheesecake. In fact, buffet food has always nauseated me, even without eating it. People eat so much I feel there should be special buffet pants for them to wear whenever they gorge themselves.

Eventually, we left the buffet with my friend overstuffed. I, on the other hand, was hungry, and couldn't wait to get home and eat some leftover quinoa.

Tamar Hirsch

IF ONLY

"There are only three things
that will heal you," said the nurse.
"Only three things:
sleep, food, and a hot shower.
Everything else is an illusion."

This was the unsolicited advice
she handed me along with my
discharge papers from a visit to the ER.
As if it were that simple.
I read what she'd handed me.
Even the discharge summary
turned a rather complex,
recurring ailment of the mind
into a two sentence paragraph.

Still, her words echoed. Three things,
sleep, food, and a hot shower
and then I'll be whole again!

If only.

Truth is, my internal sleep switch
has a short fuse, my palate and digestive tract
have constant disagreements, and the hot water
in my apartment is forever tepid.

A life like mine
cannot be so easily mended.
Trauma can shatter a life into many pieces.

Puzzles like mine can be started from the edges
or put together by an assorted pattern.
This is what I tell myself as my mind wanders
on yet another night when sleep is fleeting.

Three does not complete the puzzle.

Tamar Hirsch

RECIPE FOR ALL AROUND GOOD HEALTH

A dash of knowledge.
A pinch of 7 hours of sleep (may be hard to find).
Apply cat hugs liberally.
3 tablespoons of humor.
Gluten and dairy free vegetarian diet (not optional).

Bake with raindrops and an overcast sky.
Leave out until a good novel can accompany you.

*

This is definitely not a recipe passed down
through generations. I had to start with myself.
I embarked on my journey in August, 2013.
I added multiple components to my life.
A healthy diet and a college education
seemed to go hand in hand.
Nine months later and I am still going strong.
Now it's no longer a diet, but a way of life.
As for education, the other missing piece,
now I'm on the Dean's list and the Honor Society.
Yes, a recipe I can follow
without having to go into the kitchen.

Tamar Hirsch

SHELF AWARENESS

As a child, books were always borrowed from the library. I never had my own collection until I was an adult. My father used to say I supported the public library through late fines because even though I was a fast reader I habitually returned my assortment of books late. However, I frequently checked out the maximum amount of material allotted for children.

Thinking back now I realize I was a biblioholic at a young age, and just like an alcoholic, would go to extreme measures to fill my void. I stole my father's library card so I could check out more than fifteen books at a time. Obviously, I wasn't very clever, since fifteen-plus books is quite difficult to hide.

My addiction got out of control and soon I was hiding the evidence. As soon as any adult "vacated" their purse or wallet, I quickly scurried for their library card. In my room, the permissible books were always readily visible, while the impermissible volumes were safely hidden in various crevices.

I couldn't stop, I had no remorse, and I definitely was not going to admit my guilty pleasure and risk having to be abstinent from the written word. I continue to be a biblioholic, though as I've gotten older, I've developed shelf awareness.

Tamar Hirsch

WHAT THE FONT!? (AKA ACADEMIC THERAPY)

Through suffering, trauma, and unfortunate events, I found my voice. Well, maybe not my voice, but I certainly found a lot of pens, paper, and, lately, the Lucinda typewriter font, though occasionally I use Times New Roman or some other serif font.

Obviously, my voice masquerading as a writing implement is not the point (nor would it be if I wrote with a pencil).

Academia has done more for my mind than fifty-minute sessions in various therapist offices. In therapeutic settings I have always been an enigma; a puzzle with too many pieces missing to be put together. Looked down upon and never looked up at. Success was never even a question. An "answer" was to hope for the best but expect the worst, with the best of the worst as good as it was going to get.

Then success happened. Not only did I surprise those around me, I astonished myself. The more academics I was exposed to, the more I thrived. Somehow I started to find myself. And as my brain grew, so did my heart. I'm now able to separate people from their actions. Compassion and kindness have begun to permeate my soul. With forgiveness, I am no longer allowing my past to define me.

Now I must learn how to move in regards to stationary . . . .

Donald W. Butler

Donald was born and grew up in the Holly Park Housing Projects in Seattle. He remembers Holly Park as a violent neighborhood, overrun with drugs and crime. School was another struggle, which Donald experienced as having little to offer him. A bright spot in his teens was discovering he was gifted at dance, and for a while he became involved in various dance-related activities and performances. But Donald also became addicted to alcohol at a young age, and eventually drug- and alcohol-related crimes landed him in prison, where he spent twelve and a half years. Upon his release he began rebuilding, and recovering, his life. In prison he had become an avid reader, and as a free man began building up a book collection. He also began to write.

When I arrived at the Café to teach my first class, Donald was waiting for me. "Are you the new writing teacher?" he asked. "I'm a writer." And he shook my hand. He came to that class, and the one after, and has been a part of Safe Place from the very beginning. Donald is much loved in Safe Place where he is known as a wise soul and somewhat of a walking encyclopedia. Reading and writing and continuing to dance—these days for himself rather than an audience—are all important aspects of Donald's ongoing journey toward recovery. While life continues to have its ups and downs (as all lives do), it is never without meaning, or hope, and Donald has remained sober for many years, and describes himself as a happy man.

If I don't give away a thing I treasure,
then it's not really a gift . . .

Donald W. Butler

MY DAY WITH DAD

I only got to see my father once in my life. I was about age eight or nine years old, playing in front of my home in the Holly Park projects. I saw a tall black man in a brown suit walking down the street carrying a suitcase and eating an orange. He came closer and hugged me, then gave me a piece of the orange to eat. I had not seen him since he and my mother separated when I was an infant, but somehow I knew he was my father.

He took me to a bar in downtown Seattle and ordered some alcoholic drinks. He told me, "Don't tell your mother." I saw all of the waitresses' tip money on the table tops, and went and took it and gave it to my father. Then we went back to Holly Park, stopping at a corner grocery store along the way. My dad bought some ice cream. We went to my house, and when my mother saw my father she got very angry. "Ice cream is not food!" She yelled a lot of other things too. She could be real mean when she was angry. But she let him in anyway to spend the day with his kids.

I remember Dad put his diabetic insulin needles on top of the refrigerator, then went and played cards with my oldest brother, Joe. Dad told jokes and smiled and sang to us. He sang a blues song; some of the lyrics were: "I don't know why I love you like I do, uh huh. The mountain's high and the ocean's so blue." I don't remember too much about the rest of the day, except that in the blink of an eye he was gone. I never saw him again. He died in 1987, of cirrhosis of the liver. He drank himself to death. But part of me believes he died of a broken heart because he could not live without his wife and children. I am so glad that we even had that one day together. It made him a real person to me. I know what he looks and sounds like, how he laughs and smiles. I will never forget him. I will love my dad forever.

Donald W. Butler

JOE'S PUTT PUTT MACHINE

My oldest brother Joe was 'bout sixteen when he bought his first car. He was working at McDonald's at the time. The car was an old Toyota. A beat-up, old, red car with grey splotches all over it. My brother had to become somewhat of an auto mechanic to keep it running. Us younger kids in the family, we called his car the Putt Putt Machine.

Joe used to take us on long drives in the hot summer, down a very steep curving hill behind the Jefferson Golf Course. His radio would be tuned to a funky rhythm and blues station called KYAC.

They played songs like, "The Bertha Butt Boogie." It went, "doe, doe, doe, doe doe doe doe, doe, doe, doe . . . The party was jumping when Bertha got off her stump. Everybody was dancing and Bertha was doing the bump. They called it the Bertha Butt Boogie." Another song they played was called "The Hoochie Coo." That one went: "Do, Do, Da, Da, do, do, do do do . . . Just do what you wanna do, just as long as you hoochie coo."

I had some of the most fun times in my life, as a young child, riding around in my big brother Joe's car, the Putt Putt Machine, while listening to KYAC Radio Station.

Donald W. Butler

MOMENT IN TIME

A long time ago, I was a newspaper delivery boy in the Holly Park Housing Projects. I was about age eleven or twelve years old. I had, I believe, a dark blue delivery cart to carry the newspapers: *The Seattle Times*. Some days I delivered newspapers in the rain, with my t-shirt off. I loved it. But now, I can't stand the Seattle rain. It's too cold. My fingers freeze and my hands get ice cold because I have diabetes and my blood circulation is bad.

One morning I'd just started out on my newspaper route when I saw a cute little German Shepherd puppy on a leash, tied to the porch of a housing apartment building. He was frisky and happy, wagging his tail and moving around vigorously. His fur was beautiful shades of brown and black. I decided that I was going to take him to keep me company on my delivery route that morning. So I went up on the porch, undid his leash, and let him loose. And the puppy followed me, frolicking as I did my route.

Then, a terrible thing happened. The puppy was hit by a car as we crossed the street. It must have broken his back leg because he was limping badly. I didn't know what to do. So I took him back to the apartment porch where I got him, and put him back on his leash. When his owners got home and saw his injury, they had him put to sleep. It was one of the saddest days of my young life.

Donald W. Butler

LOST

I was about twelve years old when my mother bought me a bicycle from the Goodwill Thrift Store. It was like a 10-speed without the shifting gears, and bright orange. I used to go bike riding all over town. I called it exploring. I don't know how I found my way home sometimes. One day I got lost in downtown Seattle, near Pioneer Square, about seven miles away from my home at the Holly Park Housing Projects.

I remember I was lost and crying, and a homeless white man came to my rescue. He asked me what was wrong and I told him I was lost. He asked me what my phone numbers was. I told him: 722-1005. He bummed a quarter from a passerby and went to a phone booth to call my house and tell them where I was. My older brother Joe, about seventeen-years-old, borrowed my babysitter's car and drove downtown in her tan station wagon to get me. He gave the homeless man a couple of dollars and drove me home.

Donald W. Butler

ONE GOOD THING

I broke into an abandoned house at age ten.
The police were called. I ran out.
A police officer pulled a gun on me and yelled "Stop!"
I stopped.

Donald W. Butler

DISCOVERING THE MOONWALK

One day me, my younger brother Merle, and our friend Edward were watching television on a lazy afternoon. The musical show *American Bandstand* with Dick Clark was on, starring the rhythm and blues band Shalamar. They were all very talented street-disco type dancers. They sang and performed a very funky love song called "The Second Time Around."

Then, all of a sudden a band member named Jeffrey Daniel started to slide across the stage. It appeared that he was walking forward, but instead he was moving backward. We all were astonished by the mystical pantomime illusion. We said, "Does he have an escalator under his feet?" And, "Is he suspended by wires?" We did not know what was going on, but it turned out we were witnessing the beginning of a new dance craze. Eventually, Jeffrey taught Michael Jackson how to do the Moonwalk, and it was seen and performed by street and break dancers all over the world.

Late one night on a street corner in Holly Park Housing Projects, me and my good friend Darrel Roberts stood there discussing the latest cool dance moves. Darrel told me, "My friend Diggy taught me how to do the Moonwalk." And Darrel started Moonwalking. It looked like he was floating above the ground with sparkling stardust flying off of his feet. It was like magic. I was astonished and amazed. I asked Darrel, "Would you teach me to do it?" But Darrel stubbornly refused and said, "No."

So I set out practicing how to do it on my own. I would go up to the side of a Buddhist Temple that had reflective windows and stand on a bench and try to do the Moonwalk. After a couple of months of hard work, I figured it out. I mastered it. I copied moves from lots of other dancers, and eventually won dance contests all over town.

I got started on the contests because of a junior high school teacher, Mrs. Jessup. She looked like the singer Toni Tennille from

Captain and Tennille. She was a white woman with a skin tan, and pretty brown hair. She taught an African dance class at Sharples Junior High School. She taught me how to dance, and discovered I had an extraordinary sense of rhythm.

I won second place in a Rainier Beach Pop Locking dance contest in front of an audience of nine hundred people. I danced on an MTV commercial. I directed a music video on Group W Cable starring the Emerald City Breakers breakdancing team. And I danced on stage in the Tacoma Dome in a breakdancing contest at a Michael Jackson's *Thriller* video party in front of 14,000 people.

Donald W. Butler

FRIEND

When I was in the ninth grade at Rainier Beach High School, I had a friend named Edward Connelly. He was a very smart student in the eleventh grade doing calculus, chemistry, and physics. He was always trying to teach me something. He told me the derivative in calculus means "instantaneous velocity with the idea of limit." Many years later I learned that the integral and the derivative are opposites. The purpose of calculus is to measure rates of speed, to find the area under a curve, and to measure a tangent line to a curve.

Even though he was still in high school, Edward was tutoring students at the University of Washington. He would take several hours of physics tests with only three problems on them. Ed told me his teacher let him use the logarithm chart in the back of the math textbook and that sometimes he would have to count on his fingers. Ed said he wanted to become a physicist one day and discover the reason behind spontaneous human combustion where people are burned alive internally with no apparent cause. At the time I'd already become a teenage juvenile delinquent, alcoholic, and drug addict. Edward was not supposed to be hanging around people like me. His father was a devout Jehovah's Witness who would not let Edward drink, use drugs, or go to house parties.

Basically, me and Ed were friends because I was a good breakdancer, or pop locker, and he wanted to learn to dance. I showed him a lot of moves. By then I'd won dance contests all over Seattle, and people I taught to dance became very good also. Edward had a secret dance life he hid from his father. He was good enough to compete in dance contests but he was afraid. He learned some cool moves from some people that he taught me: the Tick, the Inch Worm, and the Colt 4S. I taught him the Tidal Wave, the Moonwalk, and the Twist to Flex.

About twenty years went by before I saw Ed again. He was a light-skinned black man who weighed about 350 pounds and looked like the Incredible Hulk. He never did become a physicist. When I asked him what type of work he did he told me he was an accountant. When I asked how much weight he could lift, bench press off his chest, he told me four hundred pounds. And that's the last time I saw him.

Donald W. Butler

PRISON

For twelve years and seven months of my early young adult life, I lived inside the Washington State prison system. It was home for me. I was institutionalized and did not believe I could function outside of prison in a normal society. I could only deal with three hot meals, a bunk bed, and being constantly supervised by police officers in a locked iron cell, day to day.

Prison days involved programming. Cleaning your cell, going to vocational class, and working in the kitchen. Things like that. Also, playing chess or ping pong, or going to the gym to lift weights, or out to the yard to play basketball. The rest of the time you're in a locked iron cell.

They feed you pretty good in jail, but when things get bad they get bad quickly, and in a bad way. People sexually assault other inmates. Prisoners sometimes kill other prisoners, and though they get caught the State does not punish them for it if they are already sentenced to life. Then there's suicide. I personally saw two people attempt suicide. One cut his own throat and the other slashed his wrists. They both lost a lot of blood, yet survived. I also tried to kill myself.

Jail could be okay or hell, it all depended.

Now I've been out of prison for longer than I was in. I love being out, and for the most part get to do what I want when I want. I love seeing things I didn't get to see in jail, like old people, or children, and cats and dogs. I love being able to go on long walks, or go to the public library or the store. I love being a free man and not getting beaten up all the time.

Donald W. Butler

OLY HARRISON

Oly was an old black prison counselor who worked the solitary confinement unit at the McNeil Island Penitentiary, where I was locked up. I got to come out of my cell in seclusion for one hour a day to talk to him. Oly was like a father to me, the father I never had. I only ever got to see my real father once. Oly looked like an old bear and had grey fuzzy eyebrows. He weighed probably around 200 pounds and he walked with a limp. He told me he'd blown out his kneecaps playing semi-pro football. As a young man he could lift 200 pounds over his head and run very fast. He was a Vietnam veteran, and stayed in the United States Air Force for thirty years. Then he became a prison guard, and eventually he became a prison counselor.

I was in solitary confinement a lot because I was a bad actor. I threw chairs at people, spit in counselors' faces, and smashed television sets. I also got in lots of fights with prison guards, even though they always won. So I'd be left in solitary to stare at the wall for months at a time. Solitary will practically drive you crazy. For two years, Oly was my personal advisor. He'd tell me, "Do you want to see the guy who caused all of your problems? Look in the mirror." He also said, "There is a helping hand at the end of your own arms."

Donald W. Butler

GOOD HEALTH

These days, being healthy means to eat several hearty and tasty meals a day. To go for a couple of several-mile walks every day. To get in a couple of sets of push-ups to keep my upper body and arms strong. To drink a lot of water and fluids to stay hydrated. Also, to abstain from illegal drugs and not drink alcoholic beverages. To abstain from smoking tobacco cigarettes, because they cause cancer. I also must get a good night's sleep so I can awaken refreshed and ready for the day. Every morning I brush my teeth and shower myself and clean myself up.

These days, I meditate every day because it calms my mind and helps maintain peace and calm. I take mental health medications to help me think before I act and be less paranoid. And at home I like to listen to music and dance around the room as this greatly relaxes me. I sing my favorite songs because that makes me happy. And every night I read books for several hours, write notes, and listen to motivational tapes. All this I do for my health.

Donald W. Butler

DANCING IN THE STREETS

Not so long ago I saw a video of people dancing. Puerto Rico was the place, and a busy street the scene, with Spanish music blaring from a live band. Older people had gathered and were dancing to the lively music. Was it the Rumba, or Samba, or even the Tango? Whatever it was, it was lively. It seemed like the people danced to live, and lived to dance.

Like Michael Jackson once said, "The dancer becomes the dance." Intoxicating rhythms, beautiful melodies, and bliss, total and complete, lost in a wonderful world of dance. Or as the singer Lionel Richie said, "they were dancing on the ceiling out there!" And that is the secret. You dance, and dance with passion. You give it all you have got and don't care who is watching you. "You shake your body down to the ground."

To dance is simple. Just listen to the music and let go. Interpret the song with your body. Dance, wiggle, and shake. You don't care who is watching. Just put on your dancing shoes and go "shake your booty."

IV

Other Voices

James Schmidt

CHANGES . . . OR CHANGELESS?

Seahawks Win. Go to Super Bowl. Okay! Celebrate!
Seahawks Lose. Don't go to Super Bowl. Okay . . .
but not okay . . . !
Meditate in silence.
It's all okay!

Money. Have all I seem to need. Just Sailing Along!
Money. Just getting by. Learning to Economize.
Do Affirmations / Prayer / Meditate in Silence.
Feeling Good!!!

Son on heroin, daughter does meth.
Sick to my stomach. Return to Meditation.
I'm okay now.

Son to Chemical Dependency Assessment.
Daughter meets with counselor / attends NA.
Big Relief. Will it last?
Return to within, to silence.
Anxiety Gone!

Learn about Addiction. Write about Addiction.
Growth of Knowledge. Bogged down in research.
Procrastinate over writing.

Self criticize. Okay . . . return to Meditation.
Warm, cozy feelings inside.
Confidence abounds!

Rent goes up $180 per month.
Anxiety is back. Do I move or stay?
Return to Meditation. All is well.
Rent goes down $180! Prayers answered.
Yea!! Appreciation. Clarity.

The New Year is here. Set Goals.
Anticipation. Meet goals. Satisfaction!
Miss goals. Disappointment.
What went wrong?
Return to Source. Meditate.
Find New Energy!! Re-evaluate.
Set new goals!
It's all okay.

Jessica Jo Wood

BLUE EYES

Recently, I read a story about the perfect way to trap a 'coon without a snare or a hound. In the story a boy places a shiny object inside a small hole. The 'coon slides his paw inside to grab the treasure, but then can't pull his paw back out. He is stuck, and by his own greed he remains trapped. His lack of wisdom leads to his doom.

Reading this my thoughts wandered back to my childhood and the time I got my hand stuck in a coin return. I reached in to check for a potential hidden treasure. Perhaps a dime or a quarter someone left behind. My hand went in fine but with a clenched fist would not come out. How does one get her hand stuck there, others might wonder. My hand was small enough to enter, too big to exit! I pulled, fighting back the urge to panic so no one would notice. Finally, someone noticed my struggle and came over to assist. Thankfully my fate wasn't like the raccoon's. I'm sure glad someone came to my rescue or I might still be there.

Cute and innocent, that was me. My baby blue eyes, glowing with the perception of innocence. Here I was, between three and four years old, playing in the front yard, pulling up handfuls of grass. I grabbed my little purse, placed my grass "money" inside, and took myself to the corner store. Noticing no one was at the counter, I walked in, still maintaining my display of perfect innocence and lost in my own pretend world. I went behind the counter and selected my purchase, placed my freshly-picked grass money on the counter, and returned home. I remained in my character of innocence. I'm just a baby playing house. I sat on the porch and began enjoying the taste of my "purchase." In less than a moment my mom appeared.

"Where did you get that?" she asked.

I responded with a big happy smile, "From the store, Mommy."

But in my heart I wondered, "How did she know?" And, "Why didn't she scold?" Hmm . . . It appeared Mom had mysteries of her own. Had she been watching from the window? Did the store person see and tell on me? Or, did she just know? I dared not ask, for some mysteries are best left unknown.

For example, years later, how did Mom know to walk up the stairs just as I took that first puff? I threw my cigarette out the window but said nothing. I asked myself again, "Why didn't she scold?" And then there was that secret I hid in my dresser drawer. One day it was gone. Did Mom take it? I'm not sure. I dared not ask. She definitely wasn't supposed to find *that*. I told my friend about the missing object and she laughed. Yes, Mom was a mystery, or was it someone higher looking after me? Maybe I could ask her, or just enjoy the fun in knowing we both thought we'd got away with something.

Melodie Clarke

GHOST

The child I once was
stands solemnly
in a corner.
Her head bowed,
shoulders slumped,
she sighs and whispers
sayings I cannot hear.

I motion for her
to come out of the corner
but she stiffens in fear.
Her head comes up
and she looks at me
with such horror,
so unprotected.

Come, I say,
holding my arms open.
And she looks at me
with questions in her eyes.
I will not hurt you, I say, quietly.
To do so will be to hurt myself.

When she runs into
my arms I gaze down
at her, rock her,
comfort her
many years too late.
My former child self,
beaten down
but not totally broken.

Hoping that by
comforting her
I will somehow
find some comfort myself,
some inner peace,
a small healing
of my inner child.

Rachel Harding

ODE TO THE TRUCK I ONCE HAD

My chariot,
my dark grey truck,
I felt like royalty
sitting in you.

You were so clean,
so tall, dependable
as the sunrise,
your ride so smooth.

It felt good
driving with my little son
in the passenger seat.
Like a better,
more legitimate, Mom.
A cool Mom even.

I felt comforted
by your bulky presence,
knowing I could take off
any time I wanted to:
knowing I didn't have to.

Knowing
you were waiting for me, patiently,
breathing on the asphalt,
always ready for another journey
over long hot desert roads
to destinations never as good
as the inside of your cab.

Rachel Harding

HAY HAIR AND SKINNED KNEES

I ran, flailing arms, hay hair.
The goats leapt in greeting.
Dipping my hands through
fast water and stalking through
the stillness of the morning forest.

My knees poked through the
ever-present holes left by my busy play.
Scabs formed and fell off like seasons.

My childhood treasures are
the memories left in the caves
that only animals remember exist.

Suzanne Star

BLACKBERRY VS. GOOD GARDEN

The big question for me is
am I safe from myself?

Egocentric to be sure
but does not one's path
to safety begin with
one's self?

There is a monster
which has taken root
inside of me.
Its name is alcoholism.

It behaves much like
blackberry plants.

Yes, blackberries are delicious, but
when it is time to plant
a good healthy garden
one must uproot the blackberry
to prevent it from smothering and choking
the good plentiful garden.

But the blackberry is nearly
impossible to get rid of.

The roots are so deep and powerful
they keep rearing up and putting forth
the same challenge again:
Do I tend my good garden
which has so much more to offer?
Or do I eat the delicious berries?

After all, rooting up the blackberry
is hard work . . . .

Tim Schooler

SELF-CARE

I watch my intake of caffeine, video-games and medications. I brush my teeth. I walk in the park. I enjoy walking for two miles. As a result of these and other beneficial elements, I receive social resilience, balanced mood, restful nights, and supportive energy.

I help as I'm able at the Recovery Café, though oversights and such are still routine. After taking a class there, I learned to not take things so personally. I'm still working on that one. Sometimes, I feel the anger in my morning pages of writing. But then I will get out of the fire of it so I am relieved.

Mostly, I have a decent amount of energy, though at times I'm still not overly functional even when I successfully follow my recipe for health. I think I'll do better as I learn to accept my limitations. I get a huge benefit from Recovery Café. I can apply myself there, and it's a flexible commitment of mine. Frequently, when I'm there, I do have energy. The Café is like the jar and my health is like my water in the jar.

V

Featured Writers

Steve Torres

Steve is a Kansas-born, second generation Mexican-American, and the eldest of five children. His family moved to Rockford, Illinois, when Steve was ten. After high school, Steve enlisted in the army, spending his basic training at Ft. Leonard Wood, Missouri, and served a tour of duty in West Germany, where he met his wife of fourteen years. After the military came college and then work as an auditor, and later in banking. After an unsuccessful marriage and divorce, Steve felt lost. Alcoholism followed.

Part of Steve's recovery journey has been discovering himself as a creative being. He came to Safe Place struggling with the idea of being a writer with a self-image of "average, with no special talents," doubtful of whether he'd ever be able to write creatively, but wanting to give it a try. That was three plus years ago. For Steve, the challenge turned out to be silencing his internal editor, that pesky little voice that told him "not good enough" before he'd even put pen to paper. And then memory and story began winning out, with wonderful results. Once let loose, Steve's writing style is flowing and articulate, and full of descriptive detail. It also reveals a deep tenderness and reverence toward all forms of life and the natural world. In addition to his writing self, Steve brings other important qualities to the group, and always listens to other people's work very carefully, and is conscientious about giving feedback and making sure no one gets left out.

Like a martial art, the pen takes the force of pain, turns it around, and disarms its dark and deadly thrust . . . .

Steve Torres

MY BROTHER TOM

. . . the one who ran miniature trucks up my arms telling me I was a highway . . .

This line from a poem by Naomi Shihab Nye about her brother evoked memories of my brother Tom, younger than me by eighteen months. I remember us taking turns running our fingers lightly over the skin on each other's arm as it tickled, soothed, and, at times, gave goose bumps. I think we were about seven and eight years old.

But we weren't always strange in that way. More often we were fighting, wrestling, calling each other "stupid," "dummy," "stink butt," and a whole assortment of other names that reflected body parts. You see, for many years Tom and I slept in the same bed, which often felt like a sardine can. If we'd each had our own sleeping bag maybe that would have ended the tussles we had over crossing the Berlin Wall that divided his side of the bed from mine, that invisible line between East and West: his side and my side with no room for negotiations or intermediaries. This was serious stuff.

Here's what it sounded like.

"Hey, your big toe is on my side."
"Don't breathe on me."
"Move your pajama sleeve back to your side."
"Your pillow is touching mine!"
"No it's not."
"Yes it is? Look! See . . ."

Then came the war over the blanket.

"It's covering more of you than me . . ."
"Is not . . ."

So here it came, tugging and pulling on the blanket. He pulled, I pulled . . . and then the sheet got out of bounds, even though the blanket was okay by then (even if close to being torn). These nightly intrusions into each other's territory finally had us falling off the bed with a deep thud, hands wrapped around each other's neck. This, unfortunately, resulted in our father's appearance, as threatening as Godzilla, fire flaming through his nostrils, eyes glaring, his voice loud enough to wake the neighbors, roaring that he was going to break our necks for us if we didn't stop it! You should have seen us then. The way Tom and I froze, suddenly as quiet and meek as lambs.

Thanks, Naomi, for sparking this memory which for the moment helps me forget the tragedy of Tom's death, thirteen years ago now, from a gunshot wound drunkenly delivered by his young, beautiful, and loving wife.

Steve Torres

BROKEN WHEELS

Only a few years ago, I was at the peak of my stuporous drinking story that now seems like a lifetime ago. My Blood Alcohol Content during those years seemed to reflect an ever-increasing gradation towards that summit of pathetic drunkenness. Blackouts, falling, stumbling, hangovers, and an easy indifference as to what I drank as long as it tasted of alcohol.

I already had one DUI, and unbeknownst to me was competently and efficiently working on my second. I don't even recall exactly what happened, except that it had that typical start at the Azteca Mexican Restaurant in Bellevue. I should say, specifically, the Azteca bar and lounge, that I had come to know so well. The patrons were like my second family and I knew all the staff, including the cooks, on a first name basis. One thing led to another or more aptly one drink led to another. By the time I had said goodnight, my memory had already become a blank. That is, until I woke up eight hours later in the Emergency Room of Evergreen Hospital.

I slowly became conscious and aware of the fact that I was not in my car. I saw a uniformed gentleman sitting at the end of the room; not a nurse, but a Kirkland police officer. I asked him where I was and what happened. When told, it all sounded like a bad, sick dream.

My car, a '92 Ford Thunderbird, had a confrontation with some electrical power generating equipment, and came out the loser. It ended upside down, with the wheels in the air and the roof crunched into the ground. The windshield was busted with glass all around. Firefighters had extricated me from the rubble through the only exit available: the windshield.

A nurse came in. I asked her what part of my body was broken or injured and she told me not a thing. No cuts, no abrasions, no concussion, no broken bones; not a scratch. My body had been so liquified that it rode the wave of the collision the way water moves with force and gravity.

Believe me, being drunk is not what I recommend for coming through an accident unhurt, and to this day I'm deeply grateful for being unscathed in a moment I could have died. But even more, I'm thankful that I did not hurt or kill someone else. That is the true blessing. I don't think I would have ever been able to live with myself if I had maimed someone or taken someone's life. I can't imagine I'd be sober now. More likely, I would still be drinking long after prison let me out.

Steve Torres

BIRCH AND THE WIZARD

Last weekend I cooked a pot of brown lentils with the help of the Vidalia Chop Wizard. It was given to me by Birch, who all of us at the Café know and love. Birch and I had been in the Café talking about cooking at home and eating healthier. I said I felt better eating almonds, seeds, apples, other fruits, vegetables, eggs, berries, oatmeal, beans, lentils and other members of the legume family. But what I didn't like, or found frustrating, was that in prepping them there was also the manual chore of cutting and chopping onions. The very thought of which at times discouraged me from actually cooking something I found totally delicious.

Birch, with his gentle, personable disposition, said he had an "As Seen On TV" onion chopper that he wasn't using and asked if I would like it. The idea of slicing and dicing my way to a fresh pot of split peas, beans and lentils, with just a few slams of the Wizard, was a thing of beauty. "Sure, whenever you can bring it in. I'll happily take it," I said.

Get this. The next day, the very next day, there was Birch and the Vidalia Chop Wizard, "As Seen On TV." He had that kind, innocent, wide-eyed look of his as he eagerly announced its arrival, holding it in his hands. Since then I have cooked three pots of pinto beans, two pots of navy beans, and four pots of lentils.

I have seen Birch several times since, and related with my own bright-eyed look what a difference that wondrous, green and white timesaver has made, and again was met with his warm and giving expression. Now life is tastier and filled with the warmest of memories thanks to Birch and the Wizard.

Steve Torres

INTO THE WOODS

Some years ago I took a five day trip to Eastern Washington with my friend Charles in his three-quarter ton truck. It was strapped with a roomy, comfortable camper, fully equipped. Everything we did was pretty much a first for me. Like target practice with a .45 caliber handgun, which practically rearranged my entire right shoulder, along with a sound so loud that it felt as if my eardrum was being kicked in. Don't think I'll do that again. Another first, and it was a big first, was pooping in the woods. Yes, Mother Nature's outhouse. When we started the trip I felt comfortable because the camper had its own commode. This is one reason I agreed to the trip.

But early on a bright sunny morning of the second day, right at the moment I needed to drop a pound or two, Charles let me know that the toilet I coveted didn't work! He admitted that if he had told me before, he'd probably be on the trip by himself. Thanks, Charles!

So off I went, toilet roll in one hand and a small shovel in the other, trying to remember exactly how he showed me it's done. How you pull down your britches and lean back against a tree. OK. I found a sturdy-looking tree, deep in the woods safe from prying eyes—which I'm so glad of because if anybody had witnessed what happened it would have made the annals of bumbling absurdity.

But the whole tree thing, which Charles had made look so easy, did not work. The tree was not cooperating, and it didn't help that I was a damned, uncoordinated city slicker. It seemed as if the tree was moving backward while I kept sliding downward. All I could see was that I'd be dropping my cargo right dab in the middle of my briefs, which were staring up at me. I gave up, gathered myself, and began desperately looking for another way with not much time to waste as Nature's call was getting louder and louder.

Then, about thirty yards away, I spotted a crooked tree with several large branches growing parallel to the ground, and about five feet above it. Bingo. My plan was to do a sort of pull-up where I could extend my legs outward and keep clear of the target area. As I reached it, I dropped my knickers hopefully for the final act, and lifted myself up as planned, praying that a hunter or huntress didn't happen by.

Lord have mercy! Balancing on that branch, while trying to focus on the business at hand, required the agility of an acrobat, which I wasn't. My legs kept drifting downward and all I could hear were my Jockeys yelling, "You're too close to the drop zone! Stay away from the drop zone! Keep clear of the drop zone!" Finally, I thought to hell with it and did the deed! When I opened my eyes I was relieved that somehow I'd accomplished my mission with clean underwear still intact. Mom would have been proud. I then put an end to it all by burying the evidence.

I could have strangled Charles when I told him: the way he laughed and laughed; and laughed. Of course, in reality I would not have touched a hair on his head, and as things turned out life had something very different in store. A year later Charles succumbed to Multiple Myeloma, a rare form of blood cancer.

So, in a way, this is a gratitude story of his friendship, and the things we did together, including the camping trip that bonded us; a memory that I always recall with a smile, as once again I hear his laughter all those years ago in the woods of Eastern Washington, where I left a part of me behind.

Steve Torres

PANHANDLING AND ME

I cannot honestly say that I can hold my head up high when I think of my recent interactions with panhandlers. On the other hand, I have never been mean, sarcastic, or rude, but mainly confused. As a member of the Café the past couple of years I've enjoyed walking south from Boren Avenue to Seattle's International District, and along the way have often been approached by those appearing to need a helping hand.

Sometimes I might see four to five people reaching out with a cup, a sign, a look, a word, a tug or an air of resignation. Each time I shake my head and say "not today" there is a part of me that doesn't feel right. I tell myself "don't be too hard on yourself. It's impractical to give to each one you meet." Often I hear the voices in my head of those who are skeptical about how these street people will use the money.

I do try to at least engage with everyone, whether it's a look of recognition, a nod, or just saying "sorry, not today." When I do give I can't always say I feel positive because I sometimes hear the other voice, the one that wonders, "did I just enable that person to abuse their body or their mind?" These encounters affect me often because I know that there are many people out there who genuinely need help, who through no fault of their own are in dire straits.

About a week ago I saw an older black man who I'd seen before in the same section of town. He was begging and approaching each passerby with the most pained and desperate look. The last time we met I didn't give him anything, and he reacted dejectedly and appeared almost tearful. This time as he came up to me I reached into my pocket and gave him $2 in change. He gave me the gentlest of smiles, said thank you, and offered to give me a hug.

How I reacted is what bothers me. I backed away from his outstretched arms and said, "this is all I have." And in that moment I feared him. Why? Because of his grimy clothes? Because of his unkempt appearance and emotional vulnerability? As I walked away the feeling of having helped him was diminished by how I had avoided him!

It's been weeks since then and I still think about it. If I had to do it again, I hope I would see the fragility and warmth of his heart and shake his hand, or give him a high five. Or maybe even give him that hug. I do wonder what is the answer. What is the way to be right with these people of the street who are all around us. I'm really searching!

Steve Torres

ON NUTHATCH TRAIL

I live in Redmond, Washington, eastward and toward the foothills, about seven miles up the hill from the town center. I really like the kind of summer we are having. If it's 80 to 90 degrees every day until October, well, that's something I'll take with me into November through March, when it's wet, cloudy, gloomy and chilly. But for right now the air is heavier, and quiet, and sound travels through it cleanly. There is a slight moistness on the skin, and the light is brighter, deeper, vaster, with an aroma of dry and tinged bark and a certain mustiness.

So last Saturday morning I decided to take an early hike and enjoy another beautiful, sunny morning. My walk took me through different terrains and various habitats, like the Redmond Watershed Preserve, Puget Sound Energy Pipeline Trail, and then back through smaller trails near Redmond Ridge, with names like Woodpecker Trail, Chickadee Trail, and Nuthatch Trail.

I was on Nuthatch Trail at mile thirteen of my seventeen mile journey when I saw something dark move about thirty yards ahead. But due to the way the trail curved and the lushness of the canopy—bushes, ferns, etc.—I didn't have a clear view, and thought maybe it was a cyclist-jogger-walker dressed in dark clothing. But as I rounded the curve I saw, disbelievingly, a black bear headed my way. It was moving at a walker's pace, and at almost the same moment I saw it, he (or she) saw me and stopped in its tracks for a second. Then, with no sound or growl, it turned around and headed back along the trail for a little ways before veering off sharply and into the bush, crashing loudly as it ran.

But by then I'd gotten a pretty good look and surmised it was a juvenile, maybe about three to three and a half feet high, and about four feet long. I guessed its weight to be around two hundred pounds.

It was definitely not a cub—which I was glad of as I wouldn't want to have met its mother—but not yet a full-grown adult.

I stood for a moment, amazed, captivated, and stunned. Had I really seen such an amazing creature at 11:40 AM on a trail I'd taken many times before? I've lived in Redmond a little over six years now, and have seen a variety of wildlife on my frequent walks, including coyotes, raccoons, bobcats, eagles, owls. But never a black bear. I felt privileged and blessed to have seen such a magnificent animal, and the next morning I went out again for another hike, using the same trails. Not necessarily to tempt fate or see another bear, but drawn by the allure of anticipating the unexpected, and to let whatever happened be as it was meant to be. I did see a couple of deer, but that was it. It's very possible that I could live where I'm at for another ten years and not ever come close to what I experienced last Saturday.

Esmeralda Hernandez

Esmeralda was born in Texas, into a large Spanish-speaking, Mexican-American family. Born with impaired vision, and other physical disabilities, Esmeralda's life was a challenge from the start. Her parents moved the family to Washington State to access more social services, and Esmeralda attended the Washington State School for the Blind from the age of eight.

In recent years, pursuing a creative path—both through writing and visual arts—has been transformative for Esmeralda, allowing her to redefine herself as an artist. Safe Place played an important role in this journey of self discovery, and for more than two years Esmeralda was an inspiring and regular presence in Safe Place. To begin with she wrote by hand in a notebook, and read out loud directly from the page by holding it very close to her face. While this was slow going, she never gave up her independence by giving her writing to someone else to read. Later on a laptop, with enlarged font size designed for people with minimal sight, made both writing and reading easier, and she blossomed further.

But over time it was visual art that most captured Esmeralda's imagination. Refusing to let herself be shut out of the visual realm, she chose instead to jump right in, using the minimal sight she does have—with its light, colors, and basic shapes—to explore painting, clay sculpture, and making collages. She is now devoting herself more fully to visual art. While we miss Esmeralda's presence in Safe Place these days, we are also cheering her on in her chosen field.

If you watch butterflies, you will see they only interact in small, short moments of safety.

Esmeralda Hernandez

OCEAN

In the heart of the city
if you listen carefully
you can hear the cries of humanity.
Each night I lie in my bed at the shelter
not knowing who will enter,
with no telling what will happen.

I have seen a sea of faces of homeless women.
As I make my way through that sea
I get to know some of them, gently pushing
my way, I make my own wave.

Some waves move forward to find land.
Some waves fold long before reaching land.

Like many, I've walked
through a sea of tears, yet still felt
God's gentle push, to remind me
that His love is wider than any ocean,
and whenever I weep He turns it into love.

Esmeralda Hernandez

HAIR

I am sure you have seen black hair from a distance. But if you look a little closer, under the golden light of the sun, you will find a precious gift of illumination that loves to show itself as a rich brownish glow. My family all have this gift, for you see our hair is not just black. Like dark wood stained until you see the lines of the wood, so is our hair.

My brother and father have soft thick hair, as soft as a carpet. My sister and I have long wavy hair. But my mother decided to venture out at the age of sixteen and color her hair blonde. And not just any old blonde. She was an original. She loved nature and the outdoors, and her hair became as blonde as the sunshine that kept her warm as she picked produce in the fields of Eastern Washington. But inside the blonde, her hair also had variations of brown to remind her of the mountain tops where she lived at times. Put together the colors were exuberant, a bright, shining glow. As she got older my mother began to curl her hair. Her hair was different, and like her personality was tough, and had volume. But running my fingers though her hair is somehow like running in an open space, and I always find confidence and strength when I am around her.

Esmeralda Hernandez

EMERALD

Emeralds are hidden under the waters of the word, preserved by the cracks of the land that shifts daily. In small increments of movement of time and pressure, they thrive under the weight of the world, and transform into something beautiful.

Though my parents did not pick me, they did pick my name. What is my name you ask? My name is Esmeralda, which in Spanish means "emerald." Little did my parents know they would have to face many pressures of the world in order for me to thrive—I was born unable to see, and unable to walk until the age of three. Until then, my parents carried me. They placed me in strollers, in their arms, and at home placed many pillows or used bean bags to help me sit up. I don't know how limp my limbs were. There were many other health issues that caused pressure for my parents and required their time to provide quality care for me. Considering my inability to walk and see, doctors decided that I would remain a vegetable for the rest of my life. I am so thankful they were incorrect with their assumptions, and so thankful my parents didn't listen to them.

We lived in Texas, and my parents spoke English as a second language. Being Spanish-speaking and living in Texas, which was and still is a poor state, made receiving benefits difficult. An important decision for my parents came from listening to a friend's advice who told them that the State of Washington had more financial benefits for children with disabilities, and how Children's Hospital in Seattle had a notable reputation for helping children with a variety of health issues. After hearing this, my parents packed their belongings and made the move from Texas to Washington.

The pressure began for me personally when I attended school. I soon fell through the cracks of mainstream education. Oftentimes,

I was left in the corner with a book or a simple worksheet to complete, while other students moved forward in their education. So my parents decided to send me to a boarding school for children with poor vision or blindness. This required me to travel four hours from home. I travelled eight hours by bus every weekend. I was about eight-years-old when I started to attend the Washington State School for the Blind (WSSB), and it was there that I became independent, learned how to walk with a cane, cook, make my bed, and accomplish other daily living skills. My parents and house parents knew that I needed to learn these skills in order to live a productive life independently.

But while going to WSSB did improve my quality of education and life, I faced more negative resistance from professional educators. Even when I managed to learn simple mathematics and enjoy reading and writing, the response from educators was often negative. Somehow they came to the conclusion that I was unable to do math. I was given an assignment to write the names of the fifty states of the U.S. in cursive, and was then informed that my writing looked like a jungle. But with time my writing did improve. While in my first year in college I learned math with the help of a tutor who spent many hours with me, writing problems in dark pencil and large numbers. Eventually, I learned algebra and logic with the help of other tutors. As a result, I obtained my Associate in Arts and Sciences Degree. Currently, I am writing creatively using my own handwriting, and editing my writing using the computer.

Like the emeralds under the sea there have been many cracks that I've fallen into. But they've only helped me to be a stronger person and become the gem I always was in my parents' eyes.

Esmeralda Hernandez

DREAM ADVICE

1.

Reach beyond your fingertips.
Let the dream become a reality,
more than something intangible.
Children live in possibilities,
and with child's faith everything is possible.
Don't let a dream become a burden.
Write it down. Keep it in a safe place.
Let it remind you
to take one day at a time, and always
keep dreaming, because you never know
which dream will come true.

2.

As an artist, I live in a world of dreams,
for without them there is no creativity.
I reach for whichever medium
will make my dreams come true.
Yes, it is my choice to walk into a dream
and capture it. My choice is to create.

Esmeralda Hernandez

SELF PORTRAIT

I tell myself, don't forget who you are.
Gentleness glides over my world as
with great precision I cautiously choose colors and words,
daily reaching for something different,
holding tightly for encouragement.
Though my eyes see dimly, what is left
is a beautiful portrait of what is to be cherished.
In the home it stands straight and tall enduring all time.
In this world there are trials,
but no one could ever tell what this portrait has endured.
It's an amazing sight that will always be remembered.

Esmeralda Hernandez

A ROSE

A rose is famous for its stem.
A butterfly is famous to the flowers below.
The beauty of creation is famous to the eyes of the beholder.
Love is a famous mystery.
Teachers are famous to their students.
It is the little things you do that make you famous.

Mary Jo El-Wattar

Mary Jo is our class elder, loved and revered for her calm and gentle presence and her wisdom. She was born and grew up up in Southern California, against the backdrop of her grandfather's orange orchards, with many happy memories and as a life-long connoisseur of oranges. But her family was also very "straight-laced" and sometimes stifling. A difficult marriage and the struggle to come to terms with her lesbian identity—and have her family accept her for who she really was—was not so happy. Meanwhile, her thirst for life and adventure refused to be contained, and included pursuing her fascination with aviation by learning to fly small aircraft. She also worked in mental health for many years as a psychiatric nurse, and later as a therapist.

Writing creatively was something Mary Jo had wanted to try for a long time, but, in contrast to flying, she lacked confidence in her abilities and the right opportunity hadn't come along yet. Safe Place provided the opportunity, with happy results. Her writing is rich in its exploration of moments, and Mary Jo, it turns out, is a master at using sensory detail. A gentle and offbeat sense of humor also frequently makes its way into her writing. But more than anything else she is an inspiring student of life, and a theme that runs through much of her work is that of aging, as she looks the end of life squarely in the face while enjoying the unexpected treasure of finding herself able to live more fully in the present.

Turn inward, light the flame. Turn inward, listen.

Mary Jo El-Wattar

THE BLUE HERON

The blue heron stands in shallow water, perfectly still. She looks at the water intently without moving at all; not one gray-blue feather moves. No wind ruffles the feathers or distracts her. I stand still, watching. I try not to move, imitating the heron, not blinking. Quick as a wink or quicker, that gorgeous bird snatches a small fish, and I watch the fish descend the heron's throat, a bulge in her neck as the fish is swallowed. Then, with an ear splitting sound that is more loud croak than bird sound, she takes off, with awkward commotion.

It is a fact: I love that heron. She saved my life. I was diagnosed with cancer. While I sat with chemicals dripping in my veins and killing blood cells, both the good ones and the cancerous ones, I pictured the blue heron, silently, patiently, standing and waiting for the right moment to dart her bill into the water to catch a fish. Instead of a fish I pictured the heron darting into my cancerous body and finding the offending cells. Thirteen years have passed since then, and she remains in my life, powerful, a symbol of health. My totem.

Mary Jo El-Wattar

NOT FAMOUS . . .

I am good at cooking, but not famous for it.
I am a good mother to my son,
and I am famous to him; only I can be his mother.
My dog, Bella, thinks I am almost everything,
but only Bella thinks this.

The blueberries I eat know I love them.
My pedicurist is happy I am her client. When she talks to me
about her little girl with a seizure disorder
I am able to give comfort.

I am good at picking up the pieces of anything broken,
pieces of broken glass or pieces of a human being.

I am very good at day dreaming.
Once, oh so long ago, a teacher threw a blackboard eraser at me
as I stared out the window, day dreaming.

I am good at saying good morning to neighbors
and strangers when I go for my early walk with Bella.
I am good at staying grounded and living my life.
I'm the only one who can do this, live my life.

I want to be like a leaf on a tree,
among the many but still singular.

Mary Jo El-Wattar

ORANGES

My grandma and grandpa lived in an orange grove in Southern California. Even my mom and dad had three orange trees in our backyard. My canary was buried under one of them, with a full ceremony, hymns and all. I would pick those fragrant and juicy oranges, bite into the skin to start the peeling process. No knife necessary. One orange was never enough. Two or three would be devoured, juice dripping off my chin.

My father raised nursery stock for the big orange growers who had orchards all over Southern California. During picking time, the ranch—Grandma and Grandpa's orchard—was filled with singing and whistling and shouting back and forth from the crew of pickers, usually from Mexico. I learned a song or two in Spanish from them, like "La Cucaracha." I didn't know that it was about a cockroach that smoked marijuana. I'd never heard of marijuana, or cockroaches for that matter.

Today, I live where I can walk to the little grocery store on the corner. I've shopped there for years, and the produce person, David, jokes with me as I pick out fruit and vegetables. When I come to the oranges I am very careful. I pick the smaller, heavier ones. I know they are heavy with juice. The big, fat ones are thick-skinned and dry in comparison. David laughs at me. I ask him, "When are you getting the Heirloom Oranges? They're the best."

We banter back and forth. Two weeks later there they are, Heirloom Oranges with the little black identification sticker proclaiming Heirloom. I take them home, three gorgeous ones fully-packed with juice. I can't wait. I use a knife now to get the peeling started. The first section tastes like home. The second section brings my backyard into view, and on I go—with the full experience of the meaning of "orange." The music of the workers, my young self among the pickers, learning the songs and a sense of community. You see, the experience is not just an orange from the store. It is a whole treasure trove of my life, my long and abundant life.

Mary Jo El-Wattar

MISTAKES

Two days after I married, way back in 1968, I realized, "Oops, I've made a mistake!" Determined to make it work I went to see a psychiatrist. He listened intently and prescribed an anti-psychotic drug: Stelazine. He forgot to mention the side effects: a stiffness like Parkinson's disease, and my tongue and throat so dry they felt like a wasteland of sand. So I had to say again, "Oops, I've made a mistake. Forget the psychiatrist." And I went home and tried to be a good wife. I even produced a child. The child, my son, was not a mistake.

Mary Jo El-Wattar

APPROACHING EIGHTY

The family I grew up with is dead.

My father. Hardworking.
Started his own business raising orange trees.
Had a short temper he learned to control . . . mmmm . . .
pretty well, though the time
he tore up a ticket in the officer's face
made the gossip round of the whole family.

My father sang, a beautiful baritone voice.
He played the cornet. He gave hard spankings,
and it was difficult for him to express love, yet
I knew, somehow, I was loved.
He smoked outside the house, and died inside the house
from emphysema, and hooked to a respirator.
He was seventy-five.

My mother. Fun-loving.
Deep feeling. Slightly hysterical.
A teacher, a singer. A giving person
who over-extended herself to others
and died of a heart attack age eighty-four.
Her heart couldn't take it.

My sister. The most recent death.
A competitor. A fierce Bible-toting
evangelical Christian, a piano player,
a singer, a wife, and mother of three.
At eighty-two she died a complicated death
involving both heart and lungs. I still grieve her.

What can I say about my own death
as I approach eighty?
I don't like being the last to die.
I would like to be remembered
as someone in love with nature.
Someone who enjoyed fresh air
and drinking from mountain streams;
the mother of a son I adore,
a respected and caring aunt to
my sister's grown children, a grandma
who always listens and is fun.
An accepting friend. One who loved life.

Mary Jo El-Wattar

BLUE ANGELS

Every year, for a long time, the Blue Angels have thundered into my presence. When I first started in AA, I heard a lot about a higher power. As a young child, God had been all-powerful and magical. So when my stuffed toy dog named Jip had his ear rubbed off by my young fingers, naturally I closed my eyes and asked God to please put Jip's ear back on. I opened my eyes and saw the ear was still gone, and I cried. That was my first crisis of faith.

When I came to AA many years later, following many crises in faith, I knew I could not have a magical God, a God that I pleaded with or bargained with. In my alcoholic thinking, I chose the Blue Angels as my higher power. After all, they were tangible, loud and uncompromising, and year after year I literally lay down when they flew over: a supplicant before the all-powerful Blue Angels.

After a few years of this, with increased abstinence and, finally, sobriety, the Blue Angels fell off the pedestal of my own making. Instead, they became symbols of war; a lure for young boys and girls to join the military, perhaps in the hope of eventually flying these powerful weapons. I became very angry with this form of recruiting our youth toward war.

Then, a number of years ago my little granddaughter was spending time with us one weekend. A Blue Angel weekend, the first weekend of August. We were outside and, since I live in the flight path, one plane was approaching from the north. It looked like it was diving for our house; I could see the pilot, he was so close. Just above us, he thrust the nose of the plane upward. A moment later a huge roar from the plane as it accelerated. Looking at my granddaughter's four-year-old face, I saw her mouth wide open and screaming. But I couldn't hear her. She and I were terrified together. It took more than a little while to become calm again.

I now call the Blue Angels the Blue Devils. I picture refugees in another country, and see a fighter plane diving at them as they try to escape down a dirt road, and my granddaughter's screams become the screams of people all over the world who are powerless in the face of sinister Blue Devils. Finding my own power has meant relinquishing both the Magical God and the God of Blue Angels, and the sense of powerlessness both generated.

Mary Jo El-Wattar

LONG TERM CARE

My son wants me to think about
long term care. What's best?
At home with visiting caregivers?
In a graduated care facility?
It is hard to think about it at all.
Yes, I'm almost eighty.
Yes, I too will die: we all do.
This is not an intellectual exercise.
This is at the heart of life,
which will end. Every day I know this.

Yet, knowing life ends
encourages me to live fully,
right now. It is because life as I know
and love it ends that I listen more closely
to the spring grumping of frogs,
the new bird in the neighborhood,
and see, really see . . . .

It is the "nitty gritty" of planning my end
that leaves me cold and confused.
The idea of "care facilities" frightens me,
the idea of being dependent on someone,
or a staff of someones.
The ideal way to die is to just drop dead.
I have hope.

Mary Jo El-Wattar

I AM THE DREAM AND THE DREAMER

My vitality is a dream come true. So is my health.
My dog, Bella, looks at me with adoring eyes
and sets her head on my knee.
Every evening I watch a family of finches take a bath,
all diving at once into the shallow container we provide.
Our garden is a delight to my eyes, a kaleidoscope
of living colors, with petunias, roses, fuchsia, and carnations.
Also the seductive fragrance of honeysuckle
and the almost-blooming jasmine.

I still have time to dream of the future.
Not necessarily mine, but the future of the world,
this earth and all its inhabitants, human and not.
This dream is like a prayer, for understanding
among nations, individuals, families, and species.
I still have time to dream of the future,
when we humans have learned reverence,
and how to act responsibly: justly.

I still have time to bless this day, to walk in sunshine
and be bowled over by the blue of the sky.
There's still time to make a sandwich to give
to the young man who hangs out at the corner grocery,
hungry: hoping for food. My hopes are no longer dramatic
as they were in my youth, but now I enjoy life
as both the dream and the dreamer.

VI

Closing Notes

PERMISSIONS AND PUBLICATION CREDITS

Donald W. Butler, "Discovering the Moonwalk," from *Raven Chronicles*, Volume 20: "Sound Tracks," 2014. Reprinted by permission of the author.

Donald W. Butler, "Joe's Putt Putt Machine," from *Raven Chronicles*, Volume 22: "Celebration," 2016. Reprinted by permission of the author.

Tamar Hirsch, "Fit For a King," from *Raven Chronicles*, Volume 21: "Laugh. Laugh? Laugh!," 2015. Reprinted by permission of the author.

Megan McInnis, "Bread," from *Raven Chronicles*, Volume 18, No. 1-2: "Why We Do What We Do," 2013. Reprinted by permission of the author.

Megan McInnis, "Finding Higher Powers, Part 1, Practicing," performed at Jet City Improv's comedy show, "Stand Up for Harm Reduction," benefit for PHRA (People's Harm Reduction Alliance), Seattle, 2015. Reprinted by permission of the author.

Bang Nguyen, "No, That's My Name . . .," from *Raven Chronicles*, Volume 21: "Laugh. Laugh? Laugh!," 2015. Reprinted by permission of the author.

Johnnie Powell, "Motown," *Raven Chronicles*, Volume 20: "Sound Tracks," 2014. Reprinted by permission of the author.

Shelby Smith, "Roll With It," published under the title "Personal Recipe for Good Health," from *Raven Chronicles*, Volume 20: "Sound Tracks," 2014. Reprinted by permission of the author.

Taumstar, "Finding My Voice," from *Raven Chronicles*, Volume 21: "Laugh. Laugh? Laugh!," 2015. Reprinted by permission of the author.

Taumstar, "Getting Older," from *Raven Chronicles*, Volume 21: "Laugh. Laugh? Laugh!," 2015. Reprinted by permission of the author.

Taumstar, "Thanksgiving on Friday?," from *Raven Chronicles*, Volume 22: "Celebration," 2016. Reprinted by permission of the author.

Angel Ybarra, "Beauty Queen," from *Raven Chronicles*, Volume 22: "Celebration," 2016. Reprinted by permission of the author.

ACKNOWLEDGMENTS

MANY PEOPLE MADE THIS BOOK AND CD POSSIBLE.

I especially wish to acknowledge the Recovery Café and the School For Recovery for their vision, love, and the wonderful home and support they have provided for Safe Place.

Thanks to 4Culture for the grant that made this project financially feasible. I also wish to thank the Jack Straw Cultural Center for a 2015 residency with the Artist Support Program. This allowed this project to explore the realm of sound, and took us into the recording studio. Special thanks to Jack Straw's very own Joan Rabinowitz and Levi Fuller for their encouragement and support. Hats off to sound engineer, Steve Ditore.

Many thanks to *Raven Chronicles* for all that they do, with special thanks to the amazing Phoebe Bosché.

Thanks to photographers Willie Pugh, for his intimate portraits of participants, and to Ginny Banks, for the cover photo. And then there are those quiet, behind-the-scenes individuals who helped make this book a reality by providing much needed feedback, typing and proofreading work: thank you Anne Frantilla, Barbara Schneider, Bevin, and, once again, Willie. Anne: my gratitude always; you've been my right-hand throughout this journey.

To everyone who has been, or is, part of Safe Place Writing Circle: I'm honored to have spent so many Friday afternoons with you. Every week you amaze and inspire me.

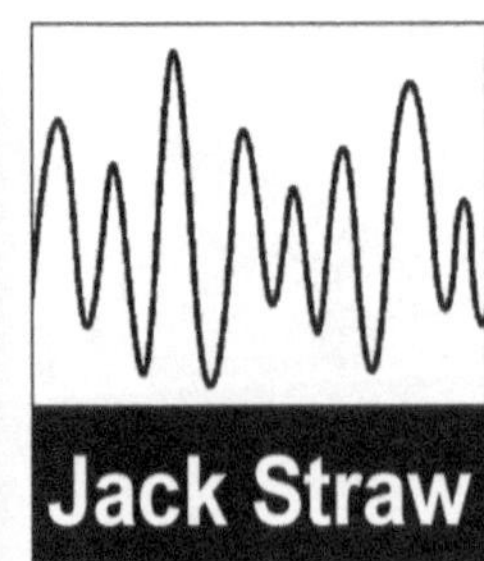

BIOGRAPHICAL NOTES

Killiam Noe

Killiam Noe is the Founding Director of Recovery Café. Before starting Recovery Café in 2004 with Ruby Takushi, Killian co-founded Samaritan Inns, a non-profit in Washington, D.C., which provides transitional and longer-term drug and alcohol free community-oriented housing for women and men recovering from homelessness, addiction, and other mental health challenges. She has written about Samaritan Inns in *Finding Our Way Home,* and about Recovery Café in *Descent Into Love.* Killian is passionate about authentic community and its power to transform.

Willie J. Pugh

Willie J. Pugh is a longtime Seattle photographer and an Alabama native. He attended an all-black high school in Selma, Alabama, during the height of the Civil Rights Movement. At age fifteen he took part in the Selma to Montgomery marches. It was during this period that he first became interested in photography as a way of recording and remembering the world in which he lived. His photos have appeared in such diverse places as *Ebony Magazine, Beacon Hill Times* and *Raven Chronicles.*

Editor's Photo: Nick Kazimir

Anna Bálint

Anna Bálint is a London-born, Seattle-based poet, writer, editor and teacher of East European descent. Her most recent editorial work is the anthology *Take a Stand: Art Against Hate* (Raven Chronicles Press, 2020). Her story collection *Horse Thief* (Curbstone Press, 2004), was a finalist for the Pacific Northwest Book Award, and her poems, stories, and essays have appeared in numerous journals and magazines. Two earlier books of poetry were *Out of the Box* and *spread them crimson sleeves like wings*. An alumna of Hedgebrook's Writers in Residence Program and the Jack Straw Writers Program, Anna has also taught creative writing for many years and in many places, including Washington State Prisons, El Centro de la Raza, Writers in the Schools, Antioch University, Richard Hugo House, and Path with Art (all in Seattle). In 2001, she received a Leading Voice Award in recognition of her creative work with urban and immigrant youth at El Centro de la Raza. Currently she is a teaching artist at Recovery Café where, in 2012, she founded Safe Place Writing Circle for people in recovery from trauma, addiction, mental illness, and homelessness.

Other Raven Books and Publications

Spirits of the Ordinary, A Tale of Casas Grandes
eBook, ISBN 987-0-9979468-6-4
Paperback, ISBN 987-0-9979468-8-8
Fiction by Kathleen Alcalá

Take a Stand: Art Against Hate, A Raven Chronicles Anthology,
(Winner of the 2021 Washington State Book Award for Poetry)
ISBN 978-0-9979468-7-1
Edited by Anna Bálint, Phoebe Bosché, Thomas Hubbard

Stealing Light, A Raven Chronicles Anthology, Selected Work 1991-1996
ISBN 978-0-9979468-5-7
Edited by Kathleen Alcalá, Phoebe Bosché, Paul Hunter, Stephanie Lawyer

Raven Chronicles Journal, Vol. 26, Last Call
ISBN 978-0-9979468-4-0
Edited by Kathleen Alcalá, Anna Bálint, Phoebe Bosché, Gary Copeland Lilley, Priscilla Long

Raven Chronicles Journal, Vol. 25, Balancing Acts
ISBN 978-0-9979468-3-3
Edited by Anna Bálint, Phoebe Bosché, Matt Briggs, Paul Hunter, Doug Johnson

Raven Chronicles Journal, Vol. 24, HOME
ISBN 978-0-9979468-2-6
Edited by Kathleen Alcalá, Anna Bálint, Phoebe Bosché, Paul Hunter, Stephanie Lawyer

Raven Chronicles Journal, Vol. 23, Jack Straw Writers Program, 1997-2016
ISBN 978-0-9979468-1-9
Edited by Phoebe Bosché, Levi Fuller, Joan Rabinowitz

www.ingramcontent.com/pod-product-compliance
Lightning Source LLC
Chambersburg PA
CBHW051922110726
47902CB00002B/375